A Damsel Productions and
Soho Theatre production

Iman Qureshi

THE MINISTRY OF
LESBIAN AFFAIRS

The Ministry of Lesbian Affairs was first performed
at Soho Theatre, London, on 6 May 2022

THE MINISTRY OF LESBIAN AFFAIRS

by Iman Qureshi

CAST

ANA	Claudia Jolly
BRIG	Mariah Louca
CONNIE	Shuna Snow
DINA	Lara Sawalha
ELLIE	Fanta Barrie
FI	Kiruna Stamell
LORI	Kibong Tanji
MAN	Fayez Bakhsh

PRODUCTION TEAM

Writer	Iman Qureshi
Director	Hannah Hauer-King
Assistant Director	Yael Elisheva
Set & Costume Designer	Anna Reid
Costume Supervisor	Danielle Levy
Lighting Designer	Zoe Spurr
Sound Designer & Co-Musical Director	Nicola T. Chang
Co-Musical Director & Vocal Coach	Victoria Calver
Assistant Musical Director	Joanna Brown
Fight Director	Maisie Carter
Casting Director	Nadine Rennie CDG
PR	Fourth Wall PR
Company Stage Manager	Saskia Godwin
Deputy Stage Manager	Kelly Evans
Assistant Stage Manager	Catherine Mizrahi
Producer	Kitty Wordsworth for Damsel Productions
Producer	Ameena Hamid for Soho Theatre

Supported by the Cara Delevingne Foundation

CAST AND CREATIVE TEAM

CLAUDIA JOLLY | ANA

Claudia trained at the Guildhall School of Music & Drama and graduated in 2016. Theatre Credits include: *Girl from the North Country* (Old Vic and West End); *The Butterfly Lion* (Chichester Festival Theatre); *The Importance of Being Earnest* (The Watermill Theatre). Claudia has worked on several productions for BBC Radio 4. Film and TV Credits include: *NW, This is Going to Hurt* (BBC); *On Chesil Beach* (BBC Film); *Matilda* (Working Title); *Pennyworth* (Warner Bros) and *Endeavour* (ITV).

MARIAH LOUCA | BRIG

Mariah's theatre credits include *Cherry Jezebel* (Everyman, Liverpool); *The Doctor* (Almeida Theatre/ATG/Adelaide Festival); *Best of Enemies* (Young Vic); *Maryland, Queer Upstairs* (Royal Court Theatre); *Tuesdays at Tesco's* (Southwark Playhouse); *All Mod Cons* (Lyric Theatre, Belfast); *Julius Caesar, Playing for Time* (Crucible Theatre); *Bumps* (Theatre503); *The Vagina Monologues* (Theatre Delicatessen) and *The Interview* (The Mono Box/PLAYSTART). Television credits include: *Eastenders, Casualty* and *Doctors* (BBC). Film credits include: *Re-displacement.*

SHUNA SNOW | CONNIE

Shuna trained at The Poor School. She's worked for the RSC, and extensively in London/UK regional theatre and BBC Radio Drama. Offie nominated Best Actress for her performance of Fay in Rona Munro's *Iron,* toured the USA with Shakespeare and an ongoing voiceover narrator for History Hit TV.

LARA SAWALHA | DINA

Lara is a British/Jordanian actor, graduating from Italia Conti Academy of Theatre Arts and is fluent in Arabic. Her theatre credits include: *Why its Kicking off Everywhere* (Young Vic, Theatre Live BBC2); *Oil* (Almeida Theatre); *Another World* (National Theatre); *Semites* (Bunker Theatre); *Nadha* (Bush Theatre). She has appeared as a series semi-regular in *Doctors* and as a guest star in *Casualty* (BBC). Lara has voiced multiple radio dramas, video games and audiobooks some of her notable credits include: *Cyberpunk 2077; Tumanbay; A Tale of Two Cities, Lullaby* and *Girls of Riyadh.*

FANTA BARRIE | ELLIE

Fanta graduated from Rose Bruford College in 2018 and went straight into *Songlines* (High Tide, Edinburgh Festival). She recently played 'Vic' in new period comedy *Belly Up* (Turbine Theatre). She is very happy to be back working with Damsel Productions once again! Other theatre credits include: *The Lovely Bones* (directed by Melly Still), *The Amber Trap* (Theatre503/Damsel productions) and *The Cereal Café* (The Other Place).

KIRUNA STAMELL | FI

Kiruna will be starring in *The Serpent Queen* for Starz later this year. During the lockdown Kiruna was busy winning the Kidscreen Award for Best On-Air Host, achieving international recognition for her work as a presenter on ABC's *Play School,* and she featured in a couple of episodes of *Brassic* (Sky TV). Kiruna was one of the original cast of the Olivier Award-winning production of *Cyrano de Bergerac,* starring James McAvoy, for The Jamie Lloyd Company, and she starred in the National Theatre of Scotland's production of *Them.* You will also recognise Kiruna from *The New Pope* (Dir. Paolo Sorrentino), *Deception/The Best Offer* (Dir. Giuseppe Tornatore),

Judy and Punch (Mirrah Foulkes); Moulin Rouge (Baz Luhrmann); Life's Too Short (Ricky Gervais); Father Brown, Holby City, All The Small Things/Heart and Soul and EastEnders (BBC) and Cast-offs (Channel 4). Kiruna has been performing across UK theatre in both classic and contemporary plays for over ten years. She has starred as Anna in the Olivier-Award-nominated production The Government Inspector for Ramps on the Moon, and performed at the National Theatre in London three times, in Everyman, directed by Rufus Norris, written by Carol Ann Duffy, movement by Javier De Frutos, and with Chiwetel Ejiofor in the title role; Tim Crouch's An Oak Tree and Richard Bean's Great Britain, which marked her West End debut.

KIBONG TANJI | LORI

Kibong is a British actor/performer based in London. She received her training from The BRIT School and has a Bachelor's Degree in Acting and Musical Theatre from the The Royal Central School of Speech and Drama. She made her West End debut playing the female cover to Arinzé Kene in Misty at Trafalgar Studios in 2018. Theatre credits include: All My Sons (Queens Theatre, Hornchurch and Tour) The Sun, The Moon and the Stars (Theatre Royal Stratford East), Tina the Musical (Aldwych Theatre). Kibong plays Lafayette in The Lair, directed by Neil Marshall, due for release in 2022.

FAYEZ BAKHSH | MAN

Fayez grew up in Reading, Berkshire to Yemeni parents. As a keen rapper, poet, martial artist and illustrator, Fayez trained as an actor graduating from Drama Studio in 2014. TV credits include: BAFTA nominated mini-series The State (Channel 4); Howard Gordon's US TV series Tyrant (FX, Sky) and a lead role in The Attack (BBC). Theatre credits include:

Tartuffe (National Theatre); Inigo, Twelfth Night (The Globe Theatre, Neuss, Germany). Film and TV credits include: Glow, Darkness; The Girl Before (HBO); Silverpoint (BBC, HULU).

IMAN QURESHI | WRITER

Iman's play The Funeral Director won the Papatango Prize in 2018 and premiered at Southwark Playhouse before touring the UK (English Touring Theatre/Papatango). Iman is currently under commission from the Bush Theatre, English Touring Theatre, the Royal Court – where she is a recipient of the Clare McIntrye Bursary – and the Almeida Theatre where she is part of the inaugural Genesis programme. She also has several TV projects in development including with STV/BBC, NBC Universal, Wychwood and ViacomCBS.

HANNAH HAUER-KING | DIRECTOR

Hannah is a London based theatre director, and Artistic Director and co-founder of Damsel Productions. She started her London directing career as Resident Assistant Director at Soho Theatre in 2014. She now works as a freelance theatre director, and has worked at venues including Kiln Theatre, Shakespeare's Globe, Soho Theatre, Southwark Playhouse, Traverse Theatre, Theatre503 and Jermyn Street Theatre. Most recent directing work includes: The Funeral Director (Southwark Playhouse & UK Tour 2019); Circle Game (Southwark Playhouse); Fabric (Soho Theatre); Call Me Fury (Hope Theatre); The Amber Trap (Theatre503); Grotty (Bunker Theatre); Fury (Soho Theatre); The Swell (Hightide Festival); Breathe (Bunker Theatre); Revolt She Said Revolt Again (Royal Central School of Speech and Drama); Clay (Pleasance Theatre); Dry Land (Jermyn Street Theatre). Associate/Assistant work: The Wife of Willesden (Kiln Theatre);

Romeo & Juliet (Shakespeare's Globe); *Radiant Vermin* (Soho Theatre) and *Daytona* (Theatre Royal Haymarket).

YAEL ELISHEVA | ASSISTANT DIRECTOR

Yael (they/them) is a director, performer and teaching artist. They are a recent RADA MA Theatre Lab graduate. Their background lies in teaching improv to incarcerated and court-involved young people with Drama Club NYC. Selected credits: *Schlepping* (RADA); *Storycourse: Pride Table* (with Adam Kantor and Benj Pasak); *A Journey of Women's Suffrage* (Rikers Island).

ANNA REID | SET & COSTUME DESIGNER

Anna is a set and costume designer based in London and a graduate of Wimbledon College of Art. Design credits include: *For Black Boys Who Have Considered Suicide When The Hue Gets Too Heavy* (New Diorama Theatre); *The Memory of Water*, *Sleepwalking*, *Cash Cow* and *The Hoes* (Hampstead Theatre); *Sessions*, *Soft Animals*, *Drip Feed*, *Fury* and *Brute* (Soho Theatre); Judith Weir's *Miss Fortune* and Gian Carlo Menotti's *The Telephone* (Guildhall School of Music and Drama); *Scrounger* (Finborough Theatre); *Midsummer Night's Dream, Our Country's Good* (Tobacco Factory Theatre); *The Sweet Science of Bruising* (Wilton's Music Hall, Southwark Playhouse); *Twelfth Night*, *Collective Rage*, *Dear Brutus*, *The Cardinal* and *School Play* (Southwark Playhouse), *Dust*, *Rasheeda Speaking* (Trafalgar Studios); *Stop Kiss* (Above the Stag); *Schism* (Park Theatre); *Grotty* (The Bunker); *Tiny Dynamite* (Old Red Lion); *Rattle Snake* (Live Theatre Newcastle, York Theatre Royal, Soho Theatre); *Four Minutes Twelve Seconds*, *The Kitchen Sink* and *Jumpers for Goalposts* (Oldham Coliseum); *Sex Worker's Opera* (set only, National Tour and Ovalhouse Theatre); *I'm Gonna Pray For You So Hard* (Finborough Theatre); *For Those Who Cry When They Hear The Foxes Scream* (Tristan Bates Theatre); *Dottir* (The Courtyard); *Mary's Babies* and *Dry Land* (Jermyn Street Theatre); *Arthur's World* (Bush Theatre); *Hippolytos* (Victoria and Albert Museum); *Hamlet* (Riverside Studios). www.annareiddesign.com

DANIELLE LEVY | COSTUME SUPERVISOR

Danielle is a London-based costumier, whose previous theatre work includes plays, West End musicals and opera, both in the UK and abroad. She holds an enhanced MA in History of Design from the Royal College of Art and V&A Museum, and BA (Hons) in Costume and Performance Design from the Arts University Bournemouth.

ZOE SPURR | LIGHTING DESIGNER

Zoe is an award-winning lighting designer. Recent work includes *Bonnie and Clyde* (West End); *Our Generation* (National Theatre/Chichester Festival Theatre); *Fantastically Great Women Who Changed the World* (Kenny Wax UK Tour); *Hamlet* (Theatre Royal Windsor); *Current, Rising* (ROH Linbury Theatre); *Wuthering Heights* (Royal Exchange Theatre) and *Emilia* (West End).

NICOLA T. CHANG | SOUND DESIGNER & CO-MUSICAL DIRECTOR

Nicola is a composer/sound designer for stage, screen and dance. Selected theatre credits include: *For Black Boys Who Have Considered Suicide When the Hue Gets Too Heavy* (Royal Court Theatre/New Diorama Theatre); *Macbeth* (Leeds Playhouse); *All Mirth and No Matter* (RSC); *Dziady* (Almeida); *White Pearl* (Royal Court Theatre) and *The Death of Ophelia* (Shakespeare's Globe).

VICTORIA CALVER | CO-MUSICAL DIRECTOR & VOCAL COACH

Victoria is a well-established Musical Director and Choral Conductor and has spent the past ten years working with many diverse and exciting professional and amateur groups. She has taught at some of London's most prestigious Performing arts colleges and currently teaches at Performance Preparation Academy in Guildford alongside running Out Of The Shadows. Victoria has performed at some of the country's finest venues and has won many choral competitions with choirs under her musical direction. She initially trained as a classical vocalist but soon discovered her passion for musical direction and found choral work, and teaching singing, incredibly rewarding.

JOANNA BROWN | ASSISTANT MUSICAL DIRECTOR

Joanna trained at Rose Bruford College, graduating with a BA (Hons) in Actor-Musicianship. She has had an accomplished and varied career as an actor, musician and musical director. Musical director credits include: *The Tempest, Little Red Riding Hood* (The Garage); *The Crucible* (Rose Theatre).

MAISIE CARTER | FIGHT DIRECTOR

Masie started her training in stage combat in her time at Guildford School of Acting. Maisie is now a fight performer, choreographer and qualified instructor with the Academy of Performance Combat. She runs her own company, MC_Combat, which strives to promote female fighters. Fight choreographer credits: *The Mountaintop* (Chipping Norton Theatre); *Lava* (Soho Theatre); *SAD* (Omnibus Theatre); *The Drifters Girl* (Garrick Theatre); *The Animal Kingdom* (Hampstead Theatre); *Fair Play* (Bush Theatre); *Malindadzimu* (Hampstead Theatre).

KITTY WORDSWORTH | PRODUCER

Kitty is a freelance theatre, comedy and screen producer. She is executive producer and co-founder of Damsel Productions. Recent theatre and comedy producer credits include: *Damsel in the Bush* (Bush Hall); *Damsel Outdoors* (various outdoor spaces); *You Stupid Darkness!* (Southwark Playhouse/Paines Plough); *Siblings* (Soho Theatre); *The Amber Trap* (Theatre503); *Fabric* (Soho Theatre and London Tour); *Grotty* (The Bunker); *Damsel Develops* (The Bunker); *Fury* (Soho Theatre); *Dry Land* (Jermyn Street Theatre); *Uncensored* (Theatre Royal Haymarket); *TABS* (workshop, Tristan Bates Theatre); *A Portobello Christmas Carol* (Tabernacle); *Snow White and the Seven Runaways* (The Tabernacle); *The Naivety: A Journey* (The Tabernacle); *Dick Whit* (The Tabernacle); *The Snow Queen* (The Tabernacle); *Peter Panto* (The Tabernacle); *Brute* (Soho Theatre) and *Juliet Cowan: Eat, Pray, Call the Police* (Live@Zedel). Associate theatre producer credits include: *What Girls Are Made Of* (Soho Theatre) and *A Level Playing Field* (Jermyn Street Theatre). Film and music video producer credits include: Shame '*Alphabet*' (dir. Tegen Williams); *Little Hard* (dir. Bel Powley and Alice Felgate); *The Last Birthday* (dir. Jaclyn Bethany); *Sunday* (dir. Daisy Stenham); *Once Upon a Time's Up* (dir. Denna Cartamkhoob). Kitty is a script reader for South of the River Pictures.

AMEENA HAMID FOR SOHO THEATRE | PRODUCER

Ameena is a London based creative producer, general manager, festival curator and facilitator. Her work focuses on increasing inclusivity and representation in theatre. She has been heralded as 'a true role model to the future generations' by Official London Theatre. Ameena was an EdFringe and British Council

Emerging Producer and one of Stage One's Bridge the Gap Producers. She is on the Board of the League of Independent Producers and part of the Creative Freelances Shaping London's Recovery Advisory Group. At just 20, Ameena earnt the accolade of youngest ever female producer in the West End as associate producer on *Death Drop* (Garrick Theatre). As theatre producer for Soho Theatre, she worked on *Shedding a Skin* by Amanda Wilkin, *curious* by Jasmine Lee-Jones, *Queens of Sheba* by Jessica L. Hagan and Ryan Calais Cameron. Other credits include: co-producer *The Wiz* (Hope Mill Theatre Manchester); general manager on *Wonderville Magic And Illusion* (Palace Theatre); assistant producer to *The Show Must Go On Live* (Palace Theatre); producer on *Graduates* at Cadogan Hall, producer on *Eating Myself* (Applecart Arts and FAE Lima, Peru); producer on *Killing It* and *Since U Been Gone* (VAULT Festival).

NADINE RENNIE CDG | CASTING DIRECTOR

Nadine was in-house casting director at Soho Theatre for over fifteen years; working on new plays by writers including Dennis Kelly, Bryony Lavery, Arinzé Kene, Roy Williams, Philip Ridley and Laura Wade. Since going freelance in January 2019, Nadine has worked for theatres across London and the UK including Arcola Theatre, Orange Tree Theatre, Sheffield Crucible, Leeds Playhouse, Fuel Theatre, National Theatre of Wales, Northern Stage, Pleasance Theatre London, Almeida and continues to cast on a regular basis for Soho Theatre. Theatre credits include: *He Said She Said* (Synergy Theatre Tour); *Bacon* (Finborough Theatre); *The Tempest* (Wildcard/Pleasance Theatre); *Britannicus* (Lyric); *The Breach* (Hampstead Theatre). TV work includes casting the first three series of BAFTA-winning series *Dixi* (CBBC).

SASKIA GODWIN | COMPANY STAGE MANAGER

Saskia trained at the Royal Academy of Dramatic Art. Credits include: *Monopoly Lifesized, The Memory of Water* (Hampstead Theatre); *Ghost Quartet* (Boulevard Theatre); *Father Christmas at the Hall* (The Royal Albert Hall); *Le Nozze di Figaro*, (The Grange Opera Festival); *Le Cid* (Dorset Opera Festival); *The Moustrap* (St Martin's Theatre); *The Mousetrap Celebrity Gala* (St Martin's Theatre).

KELLY EVANS | DEPUTY STAGE MANAGER

Kelly has been a stage manager for ten years, and a lighting biased theatre technician for thirteen years. Credits include: *Disney's The Lion King* (Lyceum Theatre); *The Drifters Girl* (Garrick Theatre); *Othello* (Dubai Opera House); *Carmen* and *Don Giovanni* (European Tour); *BBC Radio One's Teen Awards* (Wembley Arena); *Guys and Dolls* (Phoenix Theatre); *Time Flies: Celebrating 100 years of the RAF* (Theatre Royal Drury Lane); *Young Frankenstein* (Garrick Theatre); *The Toxic Avenger* (The Arts Theatre); *Petula* (National Theatre Wales Tour); *Sticky* (BRIT School); *West End Eurovision* (Dominion Theatre); *Sweet Charity* (Theatre Royal Haymarket); *Into The Woods* (Regent's Park Open Air Theatre).

CATHERINE MIZRAHI | ASSISTANT STAGE MANAGER

Catherine graduated from Bristol Old Vic Theatre School in 2018 and has been working in theatre and opera ever since. Theatre credits include: *Operation Mincemeat* (Southwark Playhouse); *Aladdin* (Venue Cymru); *Relatively Speaking* (Jermyn Street Theatre); *Family Tree* (Charlton Gardens); *La Traviata* (Opera Holland Park) and more.

DAMSEL
PRODUCTIONS

Hannah Hauer-King and Kitty Wordsworth co-founded theatre company Damsel Productions in 2015 to produce its inaugural production *Dry Land*, by Ruby Rae Spiegel, at Jermyn Street Theatre.

Damsel was set up with the key aim of developing and platforming scripts written by women, producing them with all-women creative and production teams, to help address the misrepresentation and lack of representation of women in theatre.

Damsel is intersectional in its outlook and drive, and strives to work with diverse teams of women, putting particular focus on the less-told aspects of female experiences on stage.

Damsel has produced several full-scale productions at theatres including Soho Theatre, Theatre503, the Bunker Theatre and Jermyn Street Theatre; has produced live comedy and cabaret nights; and festivals including Damsel Develops; London's first all-women directing festival; and Damsel Outdoors, a festival of commissioned new plays written for the outdoors (Damsel's answer to the pandemic closing theatre down).

www.damselproductions.co.uk | @DamselProd

Soho Theatre is London's most vibrant producer for new theatre, comedy and cabaret. We pursue creative excellence, harnessing an artistic spirit that is based in our new writing roots, the radical ethos of the fringe and the traditions of punk culture and queer performance. We champion voices that challenge from outside of the mainstream, and sometimes from within it too. We value entertainment, accessibility and enjoy a good show. We are a registered charity and social enterprise and our audiences are diverse in age, background and outlook. We are mission driven and we measure our success in:

- the NEW WORK that we produce, present and facilitate
- the CREATIVE TALENT that we nurture with artists, in our participation work and with our own staff
- the DIVERSE AUDIENCES that we play to and engage

To create theatre we nurture new playwrights, we commission new work and we produce new plays. Writers including debbie tucker green, Chris Chibnall, Theresa Ikoko and Vicky Jones had early work produced at Soho. With comedy and cabaret, we identify, develop and produce exciting new talents and present some of the biggest international stars.

We work beyond Soho taking work to and from the world's major festivals like the Edinburgh Festival Fringe. Our touring work plays across the UK and internationally with strong connections to India, Australia and the US. Our filmed comedy can be downloaded on our digital platform, seen on TV and viewed on international airlines. And, we're working towards the opening of an exciting new venue Soho Theatre Walthamstow (2023). We're ambitious, entrepreneurial and collaborative and take pride in our strong relationships with commercial partners – but the profits we make go back into supporting our work.

sohotheatre.com | www.sohotheatreondemand.com | @sohotheatre

Theo Knight
Nancy Netherwood
Jesse Phillippi
Ariella Stoian
Emily Thomson
Esosa Uwaifo
Jade Warner-Clayton
Toraigh Watson
Joanne Williams
Ally Wilson
Cara Withers
Janisha Perera
Auriella Campolina
James Darby
Thara Harrison
Chanelle King
Lee King-Brown
Fiona Nelson
Ted Riley
Robyn Wilkinson

FINANCE AND ADMINISTRATION
Head of Admin & Ops/Deputy Executive Director
  Catherine McKinney
Financial Controller Kevin Dunn
Head of Finance Gemma Beagley
Finance Assistant (Kickstart)
  Paige Miller
Facilities Manager Stuart Andrews
Admin Assistant Rebecca Dike

TECHNICAL
Head of Production Seb Cannings,
Technical & Production Manager
  Rachael Finney
Technician Kevin Millband
Technician Hannah Fullelove
Technician Lily Woodford-Lewis

SOHO THEATRE WALTHAMSTOW
Project Director Bhavita Bhatt
Artist in Residence
  Alessandro Babalola
Executive Assistant Annie Jones

SOHO THEATRE BAR
Bar Manager
Rishay Naidoo
Deputy Bar Manager
Damian Regan
Bar Supervisors
Ingrida Butkeviciute
Nejc Plemenitas
Caroline Regan
Bar Staff
Aidan Blount
Davide Costa
Genevieve Sinha
Louis Monahan
Mikhaela Oppliger Angeles
Patrick Marriott
Rachel Lonsdale
Sophie Muscat
Reuben Nehikhare
Sannidhi Jain
Sihaam Osman
Shakil Wahid
Reuben Hendy

Soho Theatre Supporters

THE MINISTRY OF LESBIAN AFFAIRS

Iman Qureshi

Acknowledgements
Iman Qureshi

It takes a village to make a play, and I am indebted to a great many people. If I have missed anyone below, I apologise. It is not for want of gratitude, but rather a writer's humble ignorance as to the epic orchestration of moving a play from page to stage.

For their thoughts on early drafts: Sarah Anderson, Mark Ravenhill, Tom Fowler, Holly Robinson, Caitlin McEwan and Margaret Perry. For the conversations on queerness which began with an internship at *Diva Magazine* in 2011 and planted the initial seeds for this play, Chance Czyzselska.

Charlotte Bennett for the initial Soho Six commission and pairing with Damsel Productions – a better match I could not have found. Everyone at Soho Theatre. Adam Brace and Gill Greer in particular for their patience and perseverance, and their endless notes on endless drafts. David Luff for taking a chance on such an ambitious play. Lakesha, Ameena, Jules, Sophie, Peter and Seb for all of your hard work and input at various stages.

Kitty Wordsworth, producer extraordinaire. Yael Elisheva whose thoughts and enthusiasm were greatly valued. The beyond-brilliant creative team for their magic: Nicola Chang, Anna Reid, Victoria Calver, Zoe Spurr, and Danielle Levy. The holy trinity of Catherine Mizrahi, Saskia Godwin and Kelly Evans – where would we be without you? Nadine Rennie for the joys of the casting process. Diana Whitehead at Fourth Wall PR for a stellar job. Nick Hern Books for the publication. The Cara Delevingne Foundation.

The cast for their amazing work, but also for making me laugh so hard, I weed my pants a little every day. Mariah Louca, Kiruna Stamell, Kibong Tanji, Claudia Jolly, Shuna Snow, Fanta Barrie, Fayez Bakhsh and Lara Sawalha – you are the absolute best.

The most wonderful agent in the world, Alex Cory, for managing my neuroses in addition to my career.

And finally – Hannah Hauer-King whom I am constantly in awe of, and who has lived and loved and breathed this play with me for three years. It would not exist without you. And I would not be me without you. Thank you for your vision, and your love.

Characters

LORI, *black, butch, late twenties/early thirties*
ANA, *white, femme, late twenties/early thirties*
DINA, *Arab, femme, late thirties*
CONNIE, *the conductor, sixties*
FI, *a wheelchair user, forties*
BRIDGET, *trans woman, fifties*
ELLIE, *woman of colour, soft butch, early twenties*

DINA'S HUSBAND
DANNY
THE DRUNK GUY AT THE BAR
HANDYMAN
One male actor, Arab, thirties, to multirole as all the male roles

A Note on Casting

All roles (bar the cis man) should be open to trans and
non-binary actors comfortable with playing women on stage.
The character of Bridget must be played by a trans woman,
and the character of Fi must be played by a disabled actor
and wheelchair user. Please cast according to the ethnicities
specified. Where none is specified this does not mean that white
is the default. It would be wonderful to have a range of body
types in the choir too.

A Note on the Chorus Lines

Dialogue has been largely assigned, but some of the Chorus
lines are left open to be allocated in rehearsal as the director
deems appropriate.

Setting

London, present day. Choir rehearsals take place on a Saturday afternoon in a run-down community centre.

Dialogue

A dash (–) at the end of a line indicates an interruption from the next speaker.

An ellipsis (…) at the end of the line indicates a trailing-off of the sentence.

A slash (/) indicates overlapping dialogue.

Square brackets [ ] indicate intended, but unspoken, words.

This text went to press before the end of rehearsals and so may differ slightly from the play as performed.

'We created our letters, our assembly, LGBTQI, fragile,
fabulous, furious, because we needed each other;
we needed to become each other's resources.
We needed each other; we need each other; we still do.'

Sara Ahmed

Prologue

*January. A space that resembles an old church or run-down
community centre. There is an outdoor patio/entrance with a
few steps up to the main hall which includes an upright piano.
A small lesbian choir begins to narrate, perhaps over the first
couple of bars of the piano intro to 'My Favourite Things' by
John Coltrane.*

CHORUS. There's a choir.

Mostly, though not exclusively

A choir of women.

A choir of women who love women.

These are not ordinary women.

These are women you do not see.

They don't appear on covers of beauty magazines

Or star in films that grace our TV screens

These are women who live on the margins.

Women to whom the world has historically denied

Dignity and visibility and pride

These are women

Who've had to fight

For space

For name

For place

For the right

To defy expectations

To live and love and thrive

And yet they must hide.

Or choose to hide.

Because sometimes that way

Life is easier.

But on Saturdays

They meet

Just a small number

Every week

In a ramshackle venue

Just off Dean Street

To sing.

The CHOIR *begins to sing of course…*

ACT ONE

Scene One

*The choir is singing a rendition of 'My Favourite Things'
with alternative lyrics. They sound good, but comical in their
sincerity and performativity, with the occasional dud note. They
are, after all, a no-audition choir of varying abilities.*

CHORUS. Feminist essays and cute rescue kittens
    Sensible footwear and vegan nutrition
    Multiple orgasms and sharing feelings
    These are a few of our favourite things

    Girls with tight buzz cuts and 'defund the police' stickers
    Short fingernails and highly skilled lickers
    The soft brush of pubic hair on my chin
    These are a few of our favourite things

    When the patriarchy bites
    When the ex-girlfriend stings
    When I'm feeling pre-menstrual
    I simply remember my favourite things
    Then I don't feel so bad!

    Perhaps halfway through the song, LORI *and* ANA *arrive
    late and listen from the entrance to the choir which continues
    to sing. They are bickering and whispering so as not to
    disturb the choir.*

ANA. See! (*Motioning to the choir.*) They've started!

LORI. I'm so hungry. Couldn't we have at least got dinner?

    ANA *rifles in her bag.*

ANA. Have a nut.

LORI. A nut? That's your solution?

ANA. Let's go in after this.

LORI. Why a lesbian choir? I hate lesbians.

ANA. You're a lesbian.

LORI. Don't remind me.

ANA. See, this is your problem.

LORI. My problem!?

ANA. Yes, your homophobia.

LORI. My homophobia?!

ANA. You don't need to repeat everything I say, it's very undermining.

LORI. Undermining?

ANA. Well you won't eat the nuts and you –

LORI. The nuts?

ANA. Yes the nuts

LORI. Give me the nuts!

> LORI *tips a portion of the nuts into her mouth – they're shouting now and do not notice that the choir has stopped singing and can easily hear the shouts.* CONNIE, *the conductor, looks crossly towards them.*

> (*Mouth full, still chewing.*) Happy?!

ANA. Course I'm not happy!

LORI. Then why am I bothering to eat your nuts –

ANA. Fine give me back my nuts!

LORI. No –

> *They tussle over the nuts as* CONNIE *interrupts, the* CHOIR *following behind.*

CONNIE. LADIES!

> ANA *and* LORI *jump and the nuts go flying everywhere. They realise everyone is staring at them.*

Are those – nuts!?

LORI. Uh...

CONNIE. This is a nut-free zone?

She points to a sign on the wall.

ELLIE. Believe it or not, that's not a metaphor.

ANA/LORI. Sorry...

They hastily begin to gather the nuts.

FI. Oh no, there are nuts everywhere now.

CONNIE. It's just that sometimes we have members with allergies.

They finish picking up the remaining nuts.

ANA. That's it I think.

CONNIE. Will you be joining us today?

BRIG. We don't bite.

ELLIE. Unless you ask nicely. (*Winks obscenely.*)

LORI. No thanks.

LORI, *furious, embarrassed, turns to leave.*

ANA. Maybe next time.

LORI *exits and* ANA *follows.*

FI. Lesbians.

BRIG. Gotta love 'em.

ELLIE. Nut-free zone. Honestly.

CONNIE (*to all the women there for choir*). Come on then. Back to practice. Thank you for those uh – unique lyrics for our warm–up, Ellie.

ELLIE. Here all day, ladies, here all day.

CONNIE. Shall we finish up that last verse before moving on to our standard repertoire?

The CHOIR *returns to singing.*

Scene Two

A week or so later. A lavish West London flat. LORI *is in her work uniform. A polo T-shirt with a company logo, knee-length shorts, boots and maybe even a bum bag. She's got a box of tools and cables and is working on a broadband line. She sings the song in the earlier scene to herself as she works.*

LORI. You've got a weak connection.

DINA (*from off*). Can you fix it?

LORI. Sure. Hardest part is spotting the problem.

DINA (*from off*). My husband really needs his sports channels.

LORI. Don't worry, I got you covered.

DINA (*enters*). Thank god. He gets really stressed otherwise. You should have seen him on holiday when he couldn't stream some football games. Did I want that holiday to be over fast. (*Hands* LORI *some water.*)

LORI. Thanks. Not many people offer you a drink in this job.

DINA. Want something stronger?

LORI. It's nine-thirty.

DINA. I won't judge. Be right back.

> DINA *leaves to pour herself a drink. We hear a pop.* LORI *carries on singing quietly.* DINA *returns, glass of champagne in hand, posing, her robe now parted to reveal a sexy negligee.*
>
> Busy day?

LORI. More of this. (*Notices* DINA*'s negligee and looks away, awkwardly.*) You?

DINA. Oh yes. I'm very busy. I'm going to put on this *Woman's Hour* programme and listen to some sad conversation about periods or FGM or fertility or menopause or sexual harassment or domestic violence and think about how great it is to be a woman. Then maybe I'll get my nails done before it's get-the-kids-from-school time, and homework-time and bath-time and bedtime, before my husband comes home and I have to work out what'll keep him in a good mood. Sometimes it's a blowjob, but most of the time it's Sky Sports, so I really, really, really need you to fix this internet.

LORI (*a beat*). So you've got kids?

DINA. Yes. You?

LORI. No.

DINA. You want them?

LORI. I'm not sure.

DINA. No, my kids, you want them?

LORI. Oh um, I'll get back to you on that. (*Beat.*) You're… American?

DINA. From Qatar. Know it?

LORI. World Cup.

DINA. Oh you like football?

LORI. Not really.

DINA. Thank god. No, I watched a lot of *Friends* growing up. The accent sticks.

LORI. How do you like London?

DINA. Four years in and I'm still working out what people do to keep warm.

LORI. Clothes help.

DINA *smiles coyly*.

DINA. So, you got a – (*Acknowledging* LORI*'s queerness pointedly.*) partner?

LORI. Yeah I do.

DINA. How long for?

LORI. Seven years or so.

DINA. Does your partner want kids?

LORI. Yeah, but I'm not ready for all that. We're thinking of getting a cat.

DINA. I'd trade my kids for a cat any day. (*Dripping with innuendo*.) You know, I've never had a woman before…

LORI. What?

DINA. Like a plumber or electrician. Usually it's some strange man coming into my house.

LORI. It's not a job a lot of women want to do, but they're trying to make it safer. There's a security thing now, where I call this number to say I've arrived and give an estimate of how long I'll be. If I don't call back in that time to say I'm out, it sends an alert.

DINA (*salaciously*). Sounds dangerous.

LORI. It's not too bad.

DINA. You look like you could handle trouble.

LORI (*finishes up what she's going*). There we go, all done.

DINA. You are?

LORI. Yeah.

DINA. And you've fixed the – connection?

LORI. Yeah. Look, these two parts basically weren't speaking to each other.

DINA. And now they are?

LORI. Yeah.

DINA. And what if it happens again?

LORI. It shouldn't but now you know how to fix it, see? Just reset this here.

DINA. And if I can't?

LORI. You can always ring the company.

DINA. Can I ask for you?

LORI. I'm kind of assigned my jobs.

DINA. What if I took your number – would you do stuff freelance?

LORI. Um…

DINA. You got much time left on your clock? The security phone thing?

LORI*'s timer beeps to indicate a 5-minute warning.*

LORI *(relieved)*. That's my five-minute warning.

DINA. I heard you singing earlier. Sounded very – sexy.

LORI. Just sign here for me please?

DINA. Are you a lesbian?

LORI. For your purposes, I'm a broadband engineer.

DINA. I think I'm a lesbian.

LORI. Oh.

DINA. And it's not because my husband's an asshole.

LORI. Right.

DINA. He is an asshole. But it's just that right now all I can think about is what it'd be like if you pushed me up against this wall right here, and –

LORI. I get it.

DINA. Where would I go if I wanted to meet other lesbians?

LORI. Um.

DINA. Like where did you meet your girlfriend?

LORI. Um I used to work at our student union when we were at uni together.

DINA. And?

LORI. For months she'd come in with her books and just stare at me.

DINA. That worked?

LORI. Well, no, then I started making her free coffees.

DINA. And that worked?

LORI. Not really. She'd just blush and say thanks.

DINA. So then?

LORI. One day she came in, completely hammered, told me I had a nice smile, wrote her number on a napkin, and ran out.

DINA. So then you called her?

LORI. Well, we texted for a while first, but yeah. Eventually we met up.

DINA. Wow, so that took like –

LORI. Six months?

DINA. Is there a fast-track system? Like I watch all these gay films about the men in parks and toilets and gyms who like just fuck complete strangers, and I want to know where to go to have that but with women.

LORI. I don't really know –

DINA. There must be clubs or bars –

LORI. I think there are a few nights but there isn't much –

DINA. Would you take me?

LORI. What about dating apps? Now your internet is working –

We hear keys in the door – a man in a suit, DINA's HUSBAND, *enters.* DINA *leaps with fear.*

HUSBAND. Don't you know what day it is?

DINA. Uh – Thursday?

HUSBAND. Yeah, and what day is Thursday?

DINA. Umm –

HUSBAND. Gym day? Ring a fucking bell?

DINA. I'm sorry, I forgot.

HUSBAND. She forgot. Now I've got to come all the way home to get my gym stuff. What's the point of you?

He ignores LORI, *grabs his gym bag from the bedroom and heads out. On his way he spots* LORI.

Hey, cable guy, could you take a look at installing a TV connection in the bathroom? Above the bath?

LORI. Sure, but you'll have to book the job in separately.

HUSBAND (*realising* LORI*'s a woman*). Oh. You're a lady! Alright. (*Laughs, then to* DINA.) Why aren't you dressed?

He leaves. LORI *and* DINA *stand in relieved silence, a moment of acknowledgement.* LORI *writes something down on a notepad.*

LORI. There's this choir. A lesbian one, my girlfriend tried to take me to. You could try that?

DINA. Would you come with me? (*A beat.*) Please?

LORI (*conflicted, then remembered how awful her husband is*). Yeah, sure.

DINA. Great! It's a date!

LORI considers refuting this, but realises it's pointless. With a shrug, she leaves.

Scene Three

A week or so after that. It's late January. We're back at choir practice, but only CONNIE *is there, boiling a kettle. It's pouring outside.* ELLIE *comes in in a waterproof, shakes it off and hangs it up.*

ELLIE. Sorry I'm late. Cats and dogs out there.

CONNIE. Where is everyone?

ELLIE. Let me see – (*Consulting her phone.*) Kim had to move her therapy, Fi's still got divorce drama, Brig said she's at a trans and non-binary poetry coffee morning, which might run over slightly, and Tamara, well she's got a new girlfriend so –

CONNIE. So?

ELLIE. You know how it goes.

CONNIE. No?

ELLIE. I give it seven years.

CONNIE. What happens after seven years?

ELLIE. Lesbian bed death. She'll come crawling back.

CONNIE. Wasn't great attendance last week either. I don't know if we can keep going like this.

ELLIE. Don't say that, Connie!

FI *enters, with* BRIG *giving her a hand with her wheelchair*

(*To* CONNIE.) There, see?

BRIG. Hello! Sorry I'm late! I was at –

CONNIE. A poetry thing, we know.

FI. Brrr. Baltic, isn't it!

BRIG (*blowing into her hands*). Not much better in here.

ELLIE. Hi-Fi. All okay?

FI. Ugh, this week has been – where does the time go, hey? When there are bills to pay, and mouths to feed and divorces to finalise. (*Her phone rings and she answers.*) Sorry, it's my son. What? (*Beat.*) No, it's the vegan salmon? To the right of the seitan steaks?

She moves off to take the call. ANA *and* LORI *enter,* CONNIE *is thrilled there are some new arrivals.*

CONNIE. Hello! Welcome! Welcome! Come in!

ELLIE. The nuts girls! Welcome back!

LORI. Uh, yeah we're waiting for a friend, maybe we'll just wait outside.

CONNIE. Nonsense, it's freezing, come in, come in. I'm Connie, the conductor.

ANA. I'm Ana.

LORI. Lori.

CONNIE. Wonderful, so glad you came back. Now, what are you, dears?

LORI. Sorry?

CONNIE. What are you?

LORI. Um, a lesbian?

CONNIE. No, soprano, or alto? High or low? Your voice?

LORI. Oh.

ANA. I'm a soprano.

CONNIE. And you?

LORI. Um low I guess?

CONNIE (*disappointed*). Yes, I suppose you look like an alto.

ANA. What does that mean?

ELLIE. She means femmes look like sopranos and butches like altos.

ANA. Quite a stereotype?

CONNIE. If you'd been doing this as long as me you'll know all stereotypes come from somewhere. Have either of you sung much before?

LORI. / A bit. /

ANA. / I was in chamber choir at school /

CONNIE. I'll get you some books.

  CONNIE *bustles off to sort the music books, while* BRIG *takes the lost-looking newbies under her wing.*

BRIG. Don't mind Connie, she's just old school, but means no harm. Cup of tea?

LORI. Yeah sure.

ELLIE. Nothing like a bit of lubrication for those vocal cords.

ANA. Is there a herbal?

ELLIE. Do we look like amateurs to you? Of course there's herbal, we've got ginger, fennel, nettle, echin… echin– what's it called again?

BRIG (*mispronounced*). Echinacea.

ANA (*correctly pronounced*). Echinacea.

CONNIE. There's no time for tea!

BRIG. Sorry.

CONNIE. T minus two minutes, ladies!

ANA (*to* LORI). Where's your closeted mum friend then?

LORI. Dunno.

CONNIE. Fi!

BRIG. Oh, Connie, I was thinking, could we sing some more pop songs? Maybe ones by fabulous queer women?

CONNIE. Like what?

BRIG. I don't know, something fun and hip. Something, you know, jazzy. Maybe like – oh I dunno, Kehlani! Or Ariana Grande?

LORI. Is she queer?

ELLIE. Don't you know, it's basically compulsory for women under thirty to identify as queer these days.

ANA. That's a bit – biphobic.

BRIG. Or queerphobic?

ELLIE. I'm not talking about bisexuals. I love bisexuals. I'm talking about straight white girls who give you googly eyes after too many glasses of prosecco at some office party and wonder what it'd be like for you to go down on them. And do they ever reciprocate? Lori? Do they?

LORI. Uh, no?

CONNIE. Can we please –

ANA nudges LORI, as if to say, don't indulge this. LORI motions 'What?!' back at her.

ELLIE. Exactly! And then they think a drunken fumble with a gold-star lesbian entitles them to walk around calling themselves queer. But you know what? They're all going to grow up, marry men, vote Tory and fuss about catchment areas like basic heteronormative bitches.

BRIG. Doesn't stop you sleeping with them.

ELLIE. Girl's gotta eat.

CONNIE. Please try not to sleep with any more new members, they're all too scared to come back after you've – had your way. Are we ready to begin, then?

FI motions one minute on the phone. DINA enters, and ELLIE sees her.

DINA. Hello, is this the lesbian choir?

LORI (*to* ANA). Ah, there she is.

CONNIE. Come in come in, yes it is –

ELLIE. Wow…

DINA. Hello, everyone!

ANA (*irritated* DINA *is so beautiful*). That's the lonely mum?!

LORI. Yeah, why?

ANA. She's not bad-looking, is she?

CONNIE (*to* DINA). We're about to start. High or low?

DINA. Is that a sex thing?

CONNIE. Just stand with the sopranos. Ellie will show you.

ELLIE. Yeah you just stand right next to me and I'll show you the ropes.

DINA. Hi, broadband girl!

LORI. You made it.

ELLIE. You know each other?

DINA. We're together!

LORI. Not together, together – not like that.

DINA. Well, kind of like that? You asked me if I'd come with you?

ANA (*indicating her and* LORI). We're together. Like a couple? You just arranged to come together.

ELLIE. Don't you love it when you come together?

DINA. Oh this is your girlfriend? You didn't say she was coming too?

CONNIE. Right, are we ready to begin? Fi! We're waiting for you!

FI. Sorry!

LORI (*to* DINA). Broadband working alright?

DINA. Sports galore.

LORI. And no trouble getting here?

DINA. I said I'm at yoga.

ELLIE. Hey have you ever tried tantric yoga?

DINA. No?

ELLIE. You wanna come with me some time?

CONNIE. Ellie!

ELLIE. What?!

CONNIE. Remember what I said about initiating new members! Fi!

FI (*on phone*). Look, I've got to go –

FI*'s son hangs up on her so she pulls the phone away, miffed.*

BRIG. All okay?

FI. Urgh, never send your children to therapy, he wants to 'process' everything!

CONNIE. Alright, everyone. Shall we get on with some singing? Given the newcomers shall we very quickly go round and do names? Loud and clear, your name, and um – a fact about yourself. I'll start. I'm Connie, and I LOVE... choir! There we go. Brig?

BRIG. Shall we do pronouns too, Connie?

CONNIE. Oh yes sorry, I keep forgetting – She-her. Brig?

BRIG. I'm Bridget, but my friends call me Brig. She-her. And I have a tattoo of an alpaca on my hip, because I love animals.

FI. I'm Fi and I'm allergic to cats. She-her.

CONNIE. Project – remember! Let's get those lungs working.

FI (*shouting*). SHE-HER in case there was any doubt.

ANA. I'm Ana. She-her. And my favourite writer is – well, it's probably a toss up between Toni Morrison and James Baldwin.

ELLIE. Ellie, she-her, And I'm – very flexible.

She lunges, viriley.

CONNIE. Thank you, Ellie. Next?

LORI. Uh – Lori, she-her.

CONNIE. And a fact, dear?

LORI. Oh. Ummm. Ummmm.

ANA. How about that your name is short for Gloria?

LORI. Why do you always do that?

ANA. What? It's a fact, isn't it?

LORI. Only my mum calls me that and I hate it.

ANA. Well, pick your own fact then.

ELLIE. Just out of interest, how long have you two been together? Seven-ish years?

ANA. How did you know that?

CONNIE. Today please!

LORI. Uh, I'm Lori, and I... like... ummm

DINA. She's really good at singing!

LORI. No, I'm –

CONNIE. That'll do! Next?!

DINA. Hi, hello, I'm Dina and I'm a she too, and a fact about me is – it's my first time at lesbian choir! And I'm excited!

CONNIE. Wonderful! Especially wonderful to see some new faces, you are all very, very welcome. Say a big welcome to the newbies!

ELL/BRIG/FI. WELCOME, NEWBIES!

Through CONNIE's *following speech an occasional drip of water from the ceiling begins to drop down on* BRIG.

CONNIE. Thank you to everyone for showing up. I know attendance has been a bit patchy, and as ever what we need is consistency. So if we could all please try to make the effort. I do this on the side of my actual job, and it takes time and love and sweat and blood and tears – not literally no, well, sometimes literally, sometimes literal tears, because – (*Getting emotional.*) this is a sacred space for us. So if you could, you know, keep up the good work!

BRIG. Connie – there's a leak?

CONNIE. Where?

BRIG. There – in the ceiling?

CONNIE. Well, no one's forcing you to stand under it.

BRIG *shifts her chair slightly.*

Good, shall we do a quick vocal warm-up? Excellent. Okay. Sing this back to me, starting with sopranos – MMMMMMM...

SOPRANOS. MMMMMMM.

CONNIE. Altos – MMMMMM....

ALTOS. MMMMMMM….

CONNIE. Gorgeous! Now MMMMMMAAAAAAAAAA

CHORUS. MMMMMMAAAAAAAA

CONNIE. AAAAAOOOOWWWWWWW

CHORUS. AAAAAOOOOWWWWWW

CONNIE. OOOOOOOWWWEEEEEEEEE

CHORUS. OOOOWWWWWEEEEEEEE

CONNIE. WE WE WE WE WE WE

CHORUS. WE WE WE WE WE WE –

CONNIE. Double time – WE WE WE WE WE WE WE

CHORUS. WE WE WE WE WE WE WE

CONNIE. WE WE WE are officially warmed up thank you
everyone!

They stop, perhaps giggle a bit.

Okay. If you get out the music I handed out last week – the
Gershwin? – I hope you've all remembered your sheets?
Save the trees. Hehe. And my printing budget. If you're
new, don't worry, I'm sure the person beside you will share.
Everyone's friendly. (*Beat.*) Can everyone see a copy?
Newbies, I know it's your first time – But go along with
it – it's easier than you think. Great, alright, everyone, let's
plough straight in.

ELLIE. Amen.

CONNIE. From the top…

ELLIE *snickers*.

(*Sternly.*) Thank you… (*Counting them in.*) Three, four –

*The song is 'I Got Rhythm' by George and Ira Gershwin,
with the pronouns swapped to queer it. They all come in
slightly out of time.* CONNIE *calls them to a halt.*

Well, that's um. Okay, let's try that again. Three, four –

*And again – bit better on time, but slightly discordant.
They're called to a halt again.*

Okay, can we all just sing the first note please.

She hits a note on the piano –

Ahhhhhhh

CHORUS (*discordant*). *AAHHHHHHH*

CONNIE (*louder*). AHHHHHH

CHORUS (*louder, trying harder but still slightly discordant*).
AHHHHHH

CONNIE (*banging the piano key hard*). AHHHHH from your
diaphragm remember!

CHORUS (*really giving it their all and nearly in tune now*).
AHHHHHHHHHHH

CONNIE. AHHHH okay, good, better. Thank you. Now from
the top. After four, one two three four –

LORI *comes in literally on four and, realising nobody is with
her, stops. She has a beautiful voice.*

Who was that? (*Beat.*) Well?

They all look at LORI *who's embarrassed and looks down.*
ANA *nudges her so she sheepishly owns up.*

LORI. Me, sorry.

CONNIE. No, that's okay, you're new. So how it works is, I
count four and then you come in after that. (*Beat.*) I don't
think you're an alto. Go stand over there.

LORI *does as she's told.*

(*To* ANA.) And you?

ANA *looks hopeful, pleased she's been singled out.*

Move down with the altos.

ANA *looks gutted.*

ANA. But…

CONNIE. Snippety snap.

ANA *moves down and* CONNIE *turns her attention back to* LORI.

Gloria, is it?

LORI. Lori.

CONNIE. Okay, Gloria, would you sing this back to me? (*Singing up a scale.*) Mary had a little baby lamb. (*Talking again.*) Go?

LORI. Uh –

CONNIE. Don't be shy –

LORI (*singing very hesitantly*). Mary had a little baby lamb.

ANA *giggles and* LORI *glares at her.*

CONNIE. And again?

LORI (*defiant now*). Mary had a little baby lamb.

Everyone is kind of blown away. LORI *stands up tall, proud. A silence.*

DINA (*smug*). I knew it.

CONNIE (*clearly thrilled but playing it cool*). Hmm. Could do a little work on the old technique, but very good. Okay, everyone, from the top of the page – ready? One, two, three, four –

They struggle through a song. It's quite a mess.

Listen to each other, you're not listening to each other!

But when they are singing it right, they sound pretty wonderful.

Scene Four

Choir practice is over and ANA *and* LORI *wait under an awning outside the hall for the rain to slow.* ANA *smokes, and glowers, embarrassed that* LORI *is so good.* ELLIE *is with them too.*

ELLIE (*to* LORI). So you've seriously not sung properly before?

LORI. Sang a bit at church when I was younger but not for ages.

ELLIE. You're amazing. Even better than Tamara.

ANA. Who's Tamara?

ELLIE. Our star soprano. But things got a bit awkward and she stopped coming

LORI. Why awkward?

ELLIE. Let's just say, where there are lesbians, there is awkward.

LORI. I don't get it.

ELLIE. Like, Tamara and I had a thing a few times, but now she's got this girlfriend, and the girlfriend's threatened by me or whatever, so she's stopped coming. Just your everyday lesbian drama.

LORI. Does that happen a lot?

ELLIE. What?

LORI. People hooking up?

ANA. Why are you so interested?

LORI. No not for me! Dina was asking where to go to hook up and I didn't know what to tell her.

ELLIE. Well, you're in the right place.

LORI. Oh no, we just want to sing.

ANA. We do, do we?

ELLIE. That's what they all say.

ANA. There are other places to hook up, why do people have to bring all that drama to a choir?

ELLIE. There's not much out there for us. You take what you can get. Think you'll come back?

LORI. / Sure /

ANA. / No / Oh?

ANA/LORI. Maybe.

They look at each other unsure.

ELLIE. I promise not to make it awkward?

ANA. That won't be necessary.

ELLIE (*nudging* ANA). This is my vow of chastity.

ANA. Really, I think we can resist you.

ELLIE. Oh! There's my bus. See you next week.

She dashes off, hood up. ANA *and* LORI *are left behind, miffed.* ANA *takes a drag on her cigarette.*

LORI. That's not good for your voice, you know.

ANA. Oh you're an expert now?

LORI. Just saying.

ANA. Well, don't just say.

LORI. Well, don't come croaking to me when your vocal cords are fucked.

ANA. Don't worry I won't. I didn't know you could sing. Why didn't you tell me?

LORI. Never came up.

ANA. You're amazing.

LORI. What's wrong?

ANA. I feel stupid. Dragging you along, telling you not to worry, that it'll be nice to make some queer friends, and everyone can sing, it's just about practice. And guess what, you're the star of the show, while I've been – demoted.

LORI. You haven't been demoted.

ANA. Oh please, everyone knows moving from soprano to alto is a demotion.

LORI. You're good at lots of other things!

ANA. Like?

LORI. Umm. Reading?

ANA. I won't be going on *Britain's Got Talent* anytime soon.

LORI. But you'd ace it on *Mastermind*! Come on! What's wrong?

ANA. Sorry, I'm just stressed. The uni still hasn't said anything about renewing my contract.

LORI. They always do, don't they?

ANA. I think they're understandably embarrassed about having only white post-colonial specialists.

LORI. It'll be fine! You'll see. You're amazing, don't you know that?

ANA. No.

LORI. Well, I do. I'm always proud of you.

ANA. Sorry I told everyone your name was Gloria.

LORI. That's alright.

ANA. We should come back to choir. If you want to.

LORI. Really?

ANA. Really.

LORI. I'd like that.

LORI *cuddles* ANA, *and* ANA *glows, happily.*

You know what I don't like? This rain.

ANA. It isn't slowing.

LORI. Make a run for it?

ANA. Come on then, what you waiting for! Come on come on come on! Race you!

ANA dashes out into the rain and LORI *chases after her.*

LORI. Such a cheat!

They squeal and laugh and tease each other as they run to get to the Tube.

Scene Five

A week later. The choir finish a song – something intense and foreboding like 'O Fortuna' from Carmina Burana. *A mug is placed under the leak. They stop singing and choir practice wraps up.*

CONNIE. Thank you very much, everyone – that's it for today.

BRIG. Connie, have you thought about my request from last week? About singing more modern songs?

CONNIE. You don't like what I pick out for us?

BRIG. No of course not, we love what you pick for us – it's just...

Looks to the others for help.

ELLIE. We hate what you pick for us!

CONNIE. Oh.

BRIG. No, no we don't hate it, we just thought we could mix it up a little?

CONNIE. We? Do you all feel this way?

FI. We love being a part of this choir, the music just wouldn't be our first choice.

CONNIE. Well, there are other choirs out there, you're welcome
to join any of them instead. This is a traditional choir.

BRIG. Doesn't mean we can't move with the times!

ELLIE. Yeah look at gay men, they're so much fun, they've got
Cher and Whitney

BRIG. And Beyoncé!

FI. While we're here singing Mahler.

BRIG. And Wagner.

FI. Could we be more dour?

BRIG. Connie, don't take this the wrong way, we really
appreciate being here and singing together –

CONNIE. And to think, I had some good news to share with you
all.

They look at each other, stumped, not wanting to hurt
CONNIE *and feeling guilty now.*

I suppose it doesn't matter now. All you care about is
Beyoncé and Jay Zed.

They all stifle giggles so as not to upset CONNIE *further.*

What?

ELLIE. Don't be like that, Connie. We were just saying, maybe
mix it up a bit!

BRIG. Exactly! Not change everything.

DINA. For the record, I don't care what we sing, I'm just happy
to be here.

ELLIE. Shhh. You're new.

FI. We really appreciate everything you do for this choir, really.

BRIG. What was your good news, Connie?

A beat as CONNIE *nurses her hurt, and determines whether
or not to let them in on the good news.*

CONNIE. Well, I had a couple of announcements. (*A dramatic pause*.) Firstly, after some long and difficult negotiations with the building management, we are finally going to have a ramp installed.

FI. Oh Connie. / Thank you!

BRIG. / About time! Brilliant news –

CONNIE. And secondly – well, I don't know how you'll feel about this now I know what you truly think about our music. But. We might be in with a shot to sing at Pride this year.

FI. On stage?!

CONNIE. Yes, the main stage!

ELLIE. Cool!

ANA. Oh brilliant!

BRIG. How did you wrangle that Connie?

CONNIE. Well, I heard they've received some complaints about the lack of lesbian inclusion, so they're proactively trying to diversify. And as we are the only lesbian choir in the country, we're a shoo-in!

LORI. Are we?!

CONNIE. What?

LORI. The only lesbian choir?

CONNIE. Yes, I googled it!

FI. Oh.

LORI. Wow.

ELLIE. That's pretty shocking.

CONNIE (*in an attempt at cheer*). The silver lining of which is that we will have no trouble getting in!

FI. Are we good enough?

CONNIE. Of course! They will be sending an organiser to come along to our practice in a few weeks to see if we've got what it takes, which we obviously do!

BRIG. Like an audition?

CONNIE. Exactly! And since our talented newbies are fast becoming regulars, I think we'll have no trouble getting the green light. Maybe we could even give Gloria a solo –

LORI. Oh I dunno –

CONNIE. What do you mean?

LORI. I don't even know if we'll be in London then.

DINA. What!?

LORI. Ana kind of lost her job so – (ANA *nudges* LORI *hard to shut up*.) / Ow!? /

ANA. / It's fine / Lori'll be here, won't you?

ANA *doesn't want to admit she's lost her job. They all look at* LORI *hopefully.* LORI *takes the cue.*

LORI. Uh yeah alright.

CONNIE. Fantastic!

DINA. Can we dress up?

ELLIE. Can I wear a suit!

BRIG. And hats! Let's all wear hats.

FI. We'll look like a lesbian barbershop choir.

BRIG. I love that idea!

ANA. Can we start calling ourselves the queer women's choir?

ELLIE. I'm so excited! Chicks dig stage presence.

DINA. Do they?

ELLIE. Oh yeah, performing is like such a pull factor.

DINA. A pull factor?

ELLIE. Yeah, it's totally going to get us laid.

DINA. Finally!

FI. Do we get paid?

CONNIE. Ladies, please, all will be discussed and decided in due course, but first we have to impress the organisers. We'll need to get our repertoire polished off and perfected – the old favourites, *Carmina*, the Gershwin.

(CONNIE *remembers their earlier request, as the choir all look nonplussed.*)

And maybe, for the final song, we could throw in some new suggestions and have a vote?

BRIG. Really?

CONNIE. Yes, really. I want you all to feel part of this choir.

BRIG. Aw thanks, Connie!

CONNIE. Okay well, that's all for today.

They begin to clear up and gather their things. ANA *pulls* LORI *aside and hisses to her.*

ANA (*to* LORI). Can you please not tell everyone I've lost my job?!

LORI (*to* ANA). What's the big deal?

ANA (*to* LORI). It's embarrassing!

ELLIE (*generally*). Hey, does anyone fancy a drink?

FI. Babysitter charges by the hour, I'm afraid.

DINA. Sorry, my husband's coming home soon.

ELLIE. Brig?

BRIG. Not tonight, sweetheart.

ELLIE. How about you two?

ANA. We're going to the cinema.

LORI. New Gillian Anderson film.

ELLIE. Nice. I've been wanting to see that. She's one of those bisexuals, right?

LORI. I hope so.

ANA. Why, think you've got a shot?

DINA. Maybe if she heard you sing, Lori.

ANA. Well, too bad, I think she's dating a man.

ELLIE. Typical. They always end up with a man.

ANA. I'm not with a man!

ELLIE. I didn't know you were / bi /

DINA. / Bye / guys! My taxi's here.

   DINA *leaves*.

ANA. Come on, we'll miss the trailers.

LORI (*to* ELLIE, *taking pity*). Hey, did you want to come?

ELLIE. Can I?

LORI. Sure.

   ELLIE *considers this – she really wants to come, but can see*
   ANA *doesn't want her to*.

ELLIE. Uh, no you lads go ahead. I'll catch up with some
   friends. My phone has been buzzing in my pocket this whole
   time, can hardly keep up with them.

ANA. Great, see you.

   ANA *practically drags* LORI *out*. ELLIE *stands around
   despondently, clearly with no one to see*. BRIG *helps* FI
   down the steps. CONNIE *watches*.

BRIG. Here let me – hopefully for the last time! Not that I mind
   obviously, because I don't, I just meant it's about time we
   have a ramp put in.

FI. I won't hold my breath. Bye, everyone.

BRIG. Bye, lovely!

   FI *leaves,* BRIG *watches her go longingly*.

CONNIE. All in good time, my dear.

BRIG. Oh god, am I that obvious?

CONNIE. They don't call me an OWL for nothing.

BRIG. An owl?

CONNIE. Older Wiser Lesbian.

BRIG. Ha. When do I qualify?

CONNIE. You, my dear, are a catch. She'd be mad not to snap
you up.

BRIG. Thanks, Connie. See you later.

   BRIG *leaves, and* CONNIE *realises* ELLIE *is still standing*
   around on her phone.

CONNIE. Oh you're still here! Everything alright?

ELLIE. Yeah. Are you hanging around for a bit?

CONNIE. No ballroom in here tonight so I thought I'd stay a
while and play.

   ELLIE *nods.*

   Would you like to sit with me?

ELLIE (*debating, not wanting to be alone*). Nah, you're alright.
See you next week.

   ELLIE *leaves.* CONNIE *sits down at the piano, and begins*
   to play.

ACT TWO

Scene One

Valentine's Day. CONNIE *is on tenterhooks about the Pride audition which is next week. It's the start of practice, and only* ELLIE *and* DINA *have arrived so far. There are now two mugs to catch drips.*

CONNIE. Didn't I tell everyone to arrive punctually today?

ELLIE. Yes you did, Connie.

CONNIE. How are we meant to get in shape for this audition if we arrive in dribs and drabs and gossip for fifteen minutes before we even get any singing in.

DINA. I've got to say, Connie, I'm here for the gossip.

CONNIE. Yes, darling, I know. Don't worry, no one is relying on you for the singing.

ELLIE. Ouch! I love it when Connie gets sassy.

DINA. Is Lori coming today?

CONNIE. She better be, I'm giving her the solo. Could you set up the chairs, please?

ELLIE *and* DINA *get the chairs out.*

ELLIE. Soooo – Dina, you doing anything tonight? For the big V-day?

DINA. My husband's travelling so I'm taking the kids to *Disney on Ice*.

ELLIE. How about tomorrow? There's this protest in the evening, if you want to come?

DINA. What are you protesting?

ELLIE. Oh you know, men, and violence and stuff. The usual.

DINA. Sounds fun, but I think he's back by then.

ELLIE. Oh no that sucks. Well, shall I give you my number just in case?

DINA. I'll go get my phone.

DINA *goes to retrieve her phone from her bag, while* CONNIE *looks on and shakes her head.*

ELLIE. Don't give me that look.

CONNIE. You know she only has eyes for one soprano, and it isn't you.

DINA *returns and* ELLIE *punches her number into her phone. Meanwhile,* BRIG *arrives for practice, and bumps into* FI, *also on her way in.*

BRIG. Ah hello! Ready for the audition next week?

FI. Oh I was born ready.

BRIG *laughs too loudly.*

BRIG. You're always so funny.

FI. I am?

BRIG. You always make me laugh.

FI. Wow. Thanks. Hey, happy Valentine's Day.

BRIG. And to you! Do you have any plans later?

FI. Oh probably just watching the episode where Tina finds out Bette's been cheating on her, and sobbing my eyes out.

BRIG. Sounds lovely. (*Plucking up the courage to ask* FI *out.*) Hey, / do you want to /

FI. / No ramp yet, I see. /

BRIG. Sorry?

FI. No ramp?

BRIG. Oh yes! Oh no! Come on, I'll give you a hand.

BRIG *helps* FI *up the steps*.

BRIG. Connie!

CONNIE. Oh good, you're both here.

BRIG. Connie, there's still no ramp.

CONNIE. Yes I'll have to speak to management. I don't know what happened.

BRIG. Fi was promised!

CONNIE. I know, I'll chase them up.

ELLIE. Hey, Fi, how's the divorce coming along?

FI. Swimmingly, thanks, Ellie.

ELLIE. All that chat about gay marriage, no one ever thought about gay divorce. How does it feel then? To be an adulteress? So Victorian!

BRIG. What?

FI. Ellie!

FI *looks to* BRIG, *not wanting her to know.* BRIG *looks surprised*.

ELLIE. Was that not common knowledge?

DINA. Would anyone like a cup of tea?

FI. Yes please!

CONNIE. There's no time for tea.

ELLIE. Not everyone's here yet, Connie.

CONNIE. Make it quick, as soon as those two arrive we're starting.

DINA *and* ELLIE *head to the kitchen, leaving* CONNIE *sorting music books, and* BRIG *and* FI *waiting*.

BRIG. I didn't realise you –

FI. Had an affair?

BRIG. Yes.

FI. What because of this chair?

BRIG. No that's not what I –

CONNIE. Thought we could sing something romantic today, in honour of Valentine's Day, what do you think?

BRIG. That's an idea.

FI (*sarcastically*). Brilliant.

CONNIE. Good! Glad you approve.

> CONNIE *returns to her books,* ELLIE *and* DINA *return and hand out teas.*

BRIG. Thanks, Ellie. Are you doing anything special for Valentine's Day?

ELLIE. Nah, I like to keep it casual. Otherwise, you get sucked into that lesbian vortex and next thing you know it's been seven years and you can't tell her North Face jacket from yours.

> ANA *and* LORI *walk in in matching North Face jackets.*

LORI. Sorry we're late!

ELLIE. See what I mean?

FI. The lesbians came in two by two –

BRIG. Hurrah, hurrah!

ANA. There's no need for that.

DINA. The lesbians came in two by two –

CHORUS. Hurrah! Hurrah! The lesbians came in two by two –

ELLIE. The butch, the femme and the ingenue

CHORUS. They all came to the choir

BRIG. To escape from the heteronormative cis-gendered capitalist bourgeoisie!

> *They all fall about laughing,*

LORI. Very funny…

ANA. Sorry, we got stuck at Ikea.

FI. Very lesbian Valentine's date.

BRIG. I do love their meatballs.

CONNIE. Are we ready to begin?

LORI. They do vegan meatballs now.

FI. Plant balls. They're not the same, they're never the same.

CONNIE. That's quite enough about balls, thank you. Danny
from the Pride committee will be here next week, and we've
got to be ready for her!

ELLIE. Have you met Danny, is she fit?

CONNIE. I have not met her, no, and I have no clue as to her
aesthetic appeal. Furthermore, we will behave with the
utmost professional decorum. Won't we, ladies?

ANA. Connie, could we be more conscientious about the
gendered language we're using?

CONNIE. Excuse me?

ANA. Ladies. That sort of thing.

BRIG. Just to be more inclusive.

ANA. And welcoming of any non-binary people.

CONNIE. Of course, of course.

DINA. Sorry, what is a non-binary?

ANA. Have you heard of Google?

LORI. Ana!

DINA. Gosh, there should be classes or something for all this.
Hey, maybe you could give me a lesson, Lori?

ELLIE. A GCSE in Lesbian. Love it. I'd get an A-star.

LORI. No, you'd get a GOLD star.

ANA *seethes, while* LORI *and* ELLIE *high-five, a bond between them forming.*

CONNIE. Yes, let's not forget we're here to sing, so if you wouldn't mind – (*Emphasising the gender neutral word.*) gang, let's crack on. Oh, and Gloria –

LORI. Lori –

CONNIE. I'm giving you the solo in this number.

LORI. What, me?

CONNIE. Yes, you. Problem?

LORI. I don't think I can –

CONNIE. Good, wonderful, thank you! Now, for our warm up – after me – Ma mi moo mi maaaaaa.

CHORUS. MA MI MOO ME MAHHHH

CONNIE. Lovely. Ah Ee Oo Ee Ahhh. PROJECT PROJECT!

CHORUS. AH EE OO EE AHHH

CONNIE. Wonderful, and one more, nice and strong here we go – la lee loo lee laa.

CHORUS. LA LEE LOO LEE LAAAA

CONNIE. Fantastic! Are we ready?

ANA. Oh, Connie, could we do some sirens please?

CONNIE. Well, if you'd arrived on time we'd have had more time for a warm-up, wouldn't we? Now, everybody, remember you sound best when you what?

CHORUS. Listen to each other.

CONNIE. Exactly! When you listen to each other. Now can everyone get out their sheets, for our final practice before we blow Danny's stockings off!

Scene Two

It's audition day in March. The choir are singing in tense unison for DANNY *from the Pride committee, who is not a woman at all, but a groomed gay man, who looks on with a faint smile. There are various receptacles on the floor to catch the drips now. The choir sings something classic like Petula Clark's 'Downtown', with* LORI *nailing her solo.* CONNIE *keeps glancing between him and the choir, getting more and more anxious, and conducting/playing the piano all the more frantically. They finish with loads of energy, perhaps do a jazz hands, but* DANNY *just smiles wanly.*

CONNIE. And that's our Petula Clark number! Now we have one more for you, chosen by popular vote –

DANNY. I think I've heard all I need for now.

CONNIE. Are you sure? Because we think this one would appeal to the younger generations, Ellie, what was this last one called again?

ELLIE. Ahem – 'Pussy is God'.

DANNY. I don't think I'm quite the right audience for that one, darling.

CONNIE. Well, thank you very much for coming to hear our little choir.

DANNY. So is this the whole choir then?

CONNIE. Er, well, we're an open choir, so depending on who shows up on the day, we sometimes have one or two more singers, don't we, ladies?

ANA *clears her throat.*

Oh sorry forgive the slip of the tongue. We're trying to use more inclusive language – so I should have said – attendance is occasionally a little higher isn't it – *gang*?

BRIG. Oh yes

ELLIE. We're usually oversubscribed.

FI. The lesbians.

ANA. And other queer women.

FI. Flock from far and wide.

LORI. To sing in our choir.

DANNY. Lovely. Now, if we do think we might want to take things forward, have you thought much about your… look… as a choir?

The choir look at themselves and each other, wondering what's wrong with their 'look'.

Outfits? Hair and make-up?

FI. We were thinking of wearing hats?

DANNY *doesn't feel this is enough…*

CONNIE. But we will give it some more thought.

DANNY. Brilliant. Glad to hear it. We'll be in touch!

CONNIE. Could everyone say a very big warm thank-you to Danny for coming to hear us sing today?

CHORUS. THANK YOU, DANNY.

A drop of water falls on DANNY*'s head. He puts his hand out and looks up.*

DANNY. Must be raining.

He leaves. As he does, the choir breathes out a collective sigh of relief.

BRIG. And that's why it's important to put pronouns on an e-signature.

FI. Danny's a bloke!

ELLIE. Danny's a cunt.

FI. Cunts are lovely, Danny's a saggy ballsack.

DINA. I like this word, cunt. So that's what you call a –

CONNIE. Let's not use genitalia to describe people, please.

BRIG. Did you see his face when the little drops of water fell on him?

DINA. Cunt. So you say this to someone you don't like?

ELLIE. Yes, but conversely you might really like their cunt.

DINA. I see.

CONNIE. Ahem, thank you.

ELLIE. Sorry.

CONNIE. Now, we're powerless over the outcome but I'm very proud of you today. And, Gloria, your solo was fantastic. On that note, choir dismissed!

They disband, and start to gather their things.

DINA. Wow, Lori, you were like, Beyoncé or something.

LORI (*flirting*). Oh yeah?

ANA (*scoffing*). Yeah, and I'm Jay-Z.

DINA. No way, can you rap?

ANA buries her face in her hands and groans.

What? Did I say something wrong?

ANA. No. It's fine.

DINA. Then what? Is that one of those British things? Like to say 'It's fine, it's fine!' when secretly you think I'm a – a – cunt?

BRIG approaches ANA, LORI and DINA having collected up some mugs.

BRIG. Any mugs?

ANA. I'm going for a smoke.

ANA, embarrassed, storms out for a cigarette. She stands outside smoking as the choir wraps up.

BRIG. Was it something I said?

DINA. I think it's me.

LORI. No, no. Sorry. She's just stressed, she's been applying for jobs and it's a bit... you know.

CONNIE *interjects as people gather their coats, etc.*

CONNIE. Perhaps we could arrange a social event for us? Do some team bonding? How about next week? Maybe we can go to that lesbian bar?

BRIG. It closed down.

CONNIE. Oh no when!?

BRIG. Last year.

CONNIE. Oh dear.

ELLIE. I know, it was the last one.

FI. Why are lesbian bars always in basements anyway?

CONNIE. We can find somewhere else?

FI. Liv's got the kids, so count me in.

BRIG. Me too.

ELLIE. Yeah same.

LORI. Sounds fun, I'm in too.

DINA. And me! I'll think of an excuse.

CONNIE. Brilliant, I'll send out a reminder on that what's happening group – is everyone a member now?

ELLIE. WhatsApp, Connie.

CONNIE. Yes, WhatsApp. Wonderful.

LORI. Here, Brig, I'll do the mugs, you always do them.

CONNIE. Thank you, Brig and Gloria. See you all next week.

BRIG. Need a hand, Fi?

FI. Don't worry, this lot'll help, just waiting for my lift.

BRIG. Bye, everyone.

ELLIE, BRIG *and* CONNIE *leave*.

DINA. Lori? I have a question. I've been on the apps like you suggested. But why is everyone so weird?

LORI *takes the mugs to the kitchen and* DINA *follows her off.* ANA *comes back in, notices* LORI *and* DINA *are nowhere to be seen, only* FI, *and looks alarmed.*

ANA. Where did they –

FI. Don't worry, they're just doing the dishes. (*Beat.*) Green-eyed monster, huh?

ANA. What?

FI. Your missus and the married Muslim.

ANA. It's like I'm invisible.

FI. Lesbian choir is where relationships go to die, don't say you weren't warned!

ANA. Great.

FI. I'm teasing.

ANA. It isn't funny. We've been together seven years and she still isn't out to her family. I thought this choir would help her accept who she is, not turn her into some lesbian choir diva.

FI. Why do you think these women come here, week after week?

ANA. To steal other people's partners?

FI. No. It's hard to accept ourselves out there. But in here, with our people, we can accept each other.

ANA. I'm not sure these are my people.

LORI *and* DINA *return*.

DINA. Look at this. This woman has a pet snake!

FI (*to* ANA). Come on, chin up. You might be surprised.

DINA. What kind of woman has a snake?!

LORI. Lesbians. (*To* ANA.) Hey, you alright?

ANA. Yeah. What are you two gabbing about?

LORI. How to tell a lesbian from a creepy man online.

FI. Ah, that old quandary.

DINA. It is just impossible to find someone normal, isn't it?

FI. Tell me about it.

LORI. I got really lucky I guess.

> LORI *puts a comforting arm around* ANA *who smiles sheepishly.*

FI (*drolly*). Very cute. Pub social next week, Connie's proposed, Ana. Team-bonding. Fancy it?

LORI. Go on, say yes.

DINA. Yes, come!

ANA. Sure, why not.

LORI. That's my girl!

> *They make to leave,* DINA *still on her dating app.*

DINA. And this woman, she wants a threesome.

ANA. That's a picture of Adriana Lima. The supermodel?

DINA. I knew she looked familiar! Is she a lesbian? Would she go out with me?

LORI. That profile is a hundred per cent guaranteed heterosexual man.

DINA. Ew. Why would they do that?!

> ANA, LORI *and* FI *all laugh knowingly. They turn out the lights as they leave, helping* FI *down the steps.*

Scene Three

It's April, the choir are having their post-rehearsal social at the pub. DINA, LORI, ANA, ELLIE, FI and BRIG. LORI and ANA are showing everyone pictures of their new cat.

LORI. And this is him sleeping, and another one of him sleeping.

ANA. But upside down this time! He loves doing that.

LORI. And oh this is him playing with a mouse.

ANA. A toy one not a real one.

ELLIE. What's his name?

ANA. Ellen.

BRIG. After Ellen…

ANA. Degeneres.

FI. A boy cat called Ellen?

ANA. Don't be so binary.

LORI. And another one of him sleeping.

ANA. Look at his little paws!

BRIG. His little face!

FI. Where did you get him?

ANA. A shelter. We're so in love.

LORI. Seriously, though, it's just like having a child.

FI. Promise you it's not.

DINA. Oh my god, that photo of you holding him, my ovaries

LORI. Oh yeah…

BRIG. That's too adorable!

DINA. Gosh look at your biceps, Lori!

BRIG. Wow.

CONNIE *returns from the loo.*

CONNIE. What are we looking at?

DINA. Lori's biceps.

ANA. Actually we were looking at pictures of our new cat.

ELLIE. How often do you work out, Lori?

LORI. Most days.

ELLIE. Yeah, same.

DINA (*to* LORI). It really shows.

CONNIE. Well, let's see the guns then?

BRIG. Connie! You dark horse!

CONNIE. What? I like a woman with a bit of muscle.

FI. Is that why Lori gets all the solos?

DINA. Come on, Lori, get the guns out!

LORI. No –

CONNIE. Yes come on then!

DINA. Please...

BRIG. Guns, guns, guns!

DINA. For me?

LORI. Oh, alright.

LORI *rolls up her sleeves and flexes her biceps.* DINA,
CONNIE *and* BRIG *all ooh and aah.*

(*Loving every second.*) I feel so objectified...

ANA. Anyway, glad you all enjoyed those. Lori, we better make
our move?

LORI. Now?

ANA. You promised.

DINA. You're leaving?!?

ANA. I have a job interview and Lori needs to help me prep.

ELLIE. What, on a Saturday?

LORI. Why don't I listen to your presentation tonight after you've practised a bit?

BRIG. Oo what's your presentation on?

LORI. Oh let me try, let me try: Post-structuralist narratives of postcolonial blackness seen through queer translocal bodies in… twenty-first century British literature? Right?

ANA nods, annoyed.

LORI. See! I'll listen to it tonight, I promise?

ANA. Fine, do what you want.

Perhaps a few of the choir members high-five and fist-pump, happy LORI *is staying.* ANA*, miffed, makes to leave, but* LORI *calls her back. As she does, a tipsy* GUY *from a nearby pool table walks past towards the bar with a pool cue in his hand.*

LORI. Aw forget it, I'll come with you.

ANA. No, stay. You're having fun.

LORI. Don't leave like that. Come here.

LORI kisses ANA on the lips. The GUY with the pool cue watches the kiss with interest.

ANA. Wow, PDA – never thought I'd see the day!

LORI. See you at home, sexy.

ANA leaves. The guy begins to watch the group from the bar with interest.

BRIG. Does anyone want a drink?

FI. A large pinot of the blanc variety, please! Liv's got the kids all weekend and I'm planning on getting trollied.

LORI. Pint for me.

ELLIE. Same.

CONNIE. Just a tonic, but could you make absolutely sure they don't add any gin?

BRIG. Sure thing. Dina?

DINA. A double Jack Daniels, please. Here let me give you some money. (*She pulls out a £50 note or two.*) Is that enough?

BRIG. I don't think they'll accept fifties, but it's okay, I've got this round. By the way I think we might be neighbours?

DINA. No way! Bayswater Road?

BRIG. Close! Porchester Terrace!

DINA. Khalas! We should hang out! I'll take you for the best falafel in Queensway!

BRIG. I'd love that!

    BRIG *leaves*.

FI. Have you heard anything about Pride yet, Connie?

CONNIE. Not yet.

FI. Shouldn't we get planning?

ELLIE. Decide on our set list!

CONNIE. Let's not tempt fate, please!

DINA. I'm so excited about going to Pride! I've never been before!

ELLIE. You're gonna love it.

DINA. My husband's away all weekend, so it should be easy-peasy!

FI. Why are you still with him again?

LORI. Yeah, he's one scary hombre, I can tell you that for nothing.

DINA. I can't just leave.

ELLIE. Do you still have feelings for him?

DINA. Of course not!

FI. Then just walk out!

DINA. I can't.

ELLIE. Why not?

FI. Are you in danger?

LORI. There are people who can help, you know –

CONNIE. Brig is a lawyer –

DINA. You don't understand! I'm here on a visa as his wife. So if I left him, I'd have to leave the country. And I can't exactly be a lesbian in Qatar. And I'd probably lose my children. So right now, this is fine. It's perfect actually.

Maybe she holds a few of their hands. Silence as they realise there isn't anything they can do to help.

CONNIE. Oh, Dina.

FI. We're here for you if you need us.

LORI. And you call me if it gets too much or anything, alright?

ELLIE. Yeah or me.

CONNIE. Let me see if Brig needs a hand.

CONNIE leaves for the bar. Only FI, LORI, ELLIE and DINA remain in the group

ELLIE. Hey, they've got a pool table! How's your game, Lori?

FI *(teasing)*. Oh, Lori's good at everything, aren't you?

LORI. Dunno about that.

DINA. Yes you are – imagine what she can do with these biceps!

DINA drapes herself on LORI, half-jokingly, and LORI laughs, enjoying the attention. The GUY at the bar catches this and decides it's time to make his move.

ELLIE. I should warn you, I'm a beast with any and all oblong objects.

LORI. Want a game?

The GUY *arrives and interrupts.*

GUY. Hey. (*A beat.*) How are you all doing today?

LORI. Um, fine thanks.

GUY. Cool – anyone want a drink?

FI. Someone's just gone to get us drinks.

GUY. Oh cool, cool. So are you girls all – friends?

ELLIE. Yeah, can we help you?

GUY. But that bird that left earlier – she was, you were together? Like a couple?

LORI. We were just going to play some pool, so –

GUY. It's winner stays on, so you'll have to beat me first.

LORI. You're not even playing right now, so can't you just let us have a game?

GUY. Sorry. Rules are rules. So are you all lesbians, then?

FI. Okay, I think you can leave us alone now.

GUY. Don't be like that. So you want to play your friend here? Friend or girlfriend? (*He winks and smiles.*)

LORI. You know what? We're fine just talking, you go ahead and play.

FI. Bye now.

GUY. No no, listen. I'll tell you what. I've got a proposition for you. If – (*Thinking what'll make the best combination for his pleasure.*) you – and – you – (*Pointing to* DINA *and* ELLIE.) have a kiss, the table's all yours.

DINA *and* ELLIE *look at each other – something shifts between them.*

LORI. Fuck off.

GUY. What?

LORI. We're just sitting here minding our own business and don't need you –

GUY. Maybe they want to!

LORI. No they don't!

ELLIE. Not for you anyway!

LORI. See? So please just fuck off.

GUY. Why are you being so rude?

LORI. I'm being rude?

GUY. Yeah, I'm just being friendly, making polite conversation. That's what people do in pubs. We are in a pub, aren't we?

FI. Well, why are you making conversation with us? There are loads of people around, why don't you go and ask those two men to kiss.

GUY. Because I don't want to see them kiss, I'm not some faggot.

DINA. Hey that's not a very nice word!

FI. We're not here to perform for you, despite what you see on the internet.

GUY. You lot are a lot fuckin' nicer on the internet, I can tell you that.

LORI. Please leave, or I'm going to complain.

GUY. Complain about what? That man over there is talking to us politely? Such bitches, you lot.

FI. Alright you can really just fuck right off, now.

GUY. No you fuck off –

He stands up tall, and approaches FI *threateningly.* LORI *hops to her feet too, to come between them, and escort him away, while* DINA *and* ELLIE *cower behind.*

LORI. Come on now –

GUY. Don't touch me, you hairy lesbian feminist bitch –

CONNIE and BRIG *arrive with the drinks and watch in stunned silence.*

FI. Oh, we're hairy bitches now are we?

LORI. Fi –

GUY. Yeah, ugly fucking lesb–

He begins to push LORI. DINA *on impulse takes a drink from* CONNIE *and throws it at him. He gasps.* DINA *instantly regrets it, screams and cowers in* ELLIE's *arms.* CONNIE *hastily steps in to de-escalate.*

CONNIE (*calmly*). That's better. Now I suggest you be on your way.

BRIG (*holding up her phone*). Or I'll call the police.

GUY. Police?! I'm the one that's been assaulted.

Defeated, the GUY *hurls the pool cue to the floor and stalks out, cursing with chilling venom.*

Fuckin' cunts I'll rip 'em in half with a kitchen knife up in their cunts, show 'em who's bein' fuckin' rude…

He leaves. The women half-laugh with nervous relief. ELLIE *and* DINA *are entwined.*

BRIG. Is everyone okay?

ELLIE. Yeah.

DINA. That was really something.

FI. What a dickhead –

FI *tries to laugh but bursts into tears.* BRIG *holds her and purrs comforting words into her ear.*

BRIG. It's alright, there, there. It's okay. He's gone. He's gone now.

The women gather round and have a group hug.

Scene Four

May. The choir is on a break. Only FI *is in the space. It's pouring again and mugs litter the floor to catch drips.* BRIG *enters, waving her phone, on cloud nine.*

BRIG. That was the restaurant confirming our reservation. You're going to love it, they grow their own vegetables, and it's all wooden tables, candles, very – (*Shyly.*) romantic.

FI (*flirtatious but also shy*). Oh really?

BRIG. Really.

FI. You look nice, by the way.

They hold hands briefly when CONNIE *bustles in.*

CONNIE. Where is every one?

FI. Kitchen I think.

CONNIE (*calling out that way*). Quickly with the pees and teas, please, we haven't got much time left

ANA, LORI, ELLIE *and* DINA *traipse back from the kitchen,* ELLIE *and* DINA *now a burgeoning couple.*

LORI. Anyone want to get a drink later?

BRIG. / Sorry /

FI. / Can't tonight /

DINA. Yeah it's our date night, we're going to a life-drawing class!

ELLIE. Baby, I just wanna draw you naked, can I?

DINA. Habibti… yes you can!

ELLIE *and* DINA *giggle and nuzzle.* LORI *a bit disappointed about being left out,* ANA *annoyed.*

ANA. Connie, where are all the mugs?

CONNIE. On the floor.

BRIG. It is a bit of a trip hazard.

LORI. And it's practically raining in here.

DINA. I think the rain is romantic.

ELLIE. Baby…

They kiss again. LORI *and* ANA *look on mutually disgusted, for different reasons.* LORI *miffed she's lost her admirer,* ANA, *annoyed that her and* LORI *never seem to be so in love.*

ANA. These leaks are getting ridiculous.

CONNIE. Oh don't remind me. And the ramp too, Fi, I'm so sorry – I have honestly sent them email after email.

FI. Welcome to my world.

CONNIE. I'll get it sorted if it's the last thing I do. Now, are we ready?

The choir mosey back to their seats for a final song.

BRIG. Oh, did you hear back on that interview, Ana?

ANA. Not yet.

BRIG. Fingers crossed for you!

LORI *and* ANA *exchange an awkward look.*

What?

LORI. The job's in Exeter.

BRIG. Oh no…

CONNIE. Right! Before we crack on, I had a little bit of news to share with you

ELLIE. Oh my god it's about Pride, isn't it?

BRIG. Oh please say it's good news.

LORI. It will be, we were great!

FI. I bet you it's a no.

DINA. No!

CONNIE. If you all stop talking at once I can put you out of your misery!

A dramatic silence.

ELLIE. Well go on then, Connie!

CONNIE. I'm very sorry to say, my friends – that we're going to need a name for our choir because you are looking at the new opening act for the Pride mainstage!

The choir erupt into a gaggle of excited cheers and hugs.

LORI. That's amazing!

ELLIE. I can't believe it

FI. I thought we already had a name?

CONNIE. Long ago when this choir was founded it was called Sing Out. But I think it's time for a change, to reflect this new stage in our herstory!

BRIG. That's a wonderful idea!

DINA. I like Sing Out.

CONNIE. Oh, I think we can be more fun than that – come on, let's be creative?

ELLIE. Oh, oh, oh – lesbi creative?

FI. That sounds like a lesbian performance art group.

ELLIE. Ouch.

LORI. Oh, I know – how about the tonedykes?

ANA. Dyke isn't very inclusive.

ELLIE. Why not? I'm a dyke.

DINA. And I love dykes.

ANA. Remember I suggested the queer women's choir?

ELLIE. Snoozefest.

FI. What about the Lescendos? (*Explaining*.) Like crescendo, but – Lescendo?

LORI. It doesn't work if it needs explaining.

ELLIE. The Lesbian Players?

CONNIE. I like that!

ANA. No.

BRIG. What about the Lesbian Chanteuses?

ANA. Oh, the Queer Chanteuses?

LORI. The Lesbian Mafia?

FI. The Lesbian Ministry?

ANA. Not all of us are lesbians!

BRIG. I've got it, I've got it – The Ministry of Lesbian Affairs!

FI. Oooh, now I like that!

BRIG. You do!?

DINA. Cool!

LORI. I love it!

ANA. It is witty, I suppose.

ELLIE. Yeah that's pretty badass.

CONNIE. Well, Pride London – get ready for the Ministry of Lesbian Affairs!

They all look delighted with themselves.

CONNIE. Now, shall we finish up with the Tracy? I do love this number, thank you for the suggestion, Brig. Though I should say, this is really from my generation, back when I was a wild young thing marching and protesting in Doc Martens.

DINA. Connie, that sounds so sexy! You'll have to show us pictures!

CONNIE. If you're good, maybe I will. Now, Dina, my dear – I'd like you to take the melody on this today? How about that?

DINA. Me?!

CONNIE. Indeed.

DINA. Wallahi? Oh wow!

CONNIE. Everyone ready? Okay. Two three four –

DINA *begins, and they gradually come in. The song is Tracy Chapman's 'Talkin' Bout a Revolution'.*

The choir breaks to get their coats and bags. BRIG *pulls flowers from her bag for* FI *and they go off on their date.*

Interval.

ACT THREE

Scene One

June. Pride. The choir are singing 'Pussy is God' by King Princess. This merges into them speaking:

CHORUS. Why it happened, we can't say

But we know what happened

And we know how it happened

The who, too, we know.

This is how it all went down.

It was Pride

Rainbows were flying high

And even though it was raining on our parade

No one cared

We were all out with our pink and our gold and our multicoloured hair

And our leather

And our check

And our fades

And our kicks

And our dresses

And our tresses

And our lovers

And our lovers' lovers

And our ex-lovers

And our lovers' ex-lovers

Who are now our lovers

And our gays

And our gals

And our non-binary pals

With the shame packed away

For just one day

Because today we were out and loud and proud

And we had an early slot

And the crowds were still sober

And smiling

And eager

And we were ready

And rehearsed

And warmed up

And looking fly

And we were so glad to be part of it all

And we had a moment

Just before the moment we began

When we could see

This sea

Of LGB&T

Just waiting

And smiling

And feeling good about themselves

And about us

And it felt like we were the majority

The A-listers

Or royalty

Like we were part of history

No longer invisible

We were always here

This assembly of queers

We were at Stonewall

With Stormé DeLarverie

Or even before then, with Radclyffe Hall

And Susan Sontag and Audre Lorde

We were Billie Holiday

And Dusty Springfield

Eleanor Roosevelt

And Lorraine Hansberry

We were Vita and Virginia

And Emily Dickinson

Alice B Toklas and Gertrude Stein

Leslie Feinberg

And Lena Waithe

And Hayley Kiyoko – our very own Lesbian Jesus

We were

The Dykes To Watch Out For

And many, many more

Whose names will be lost to lesbian invisibility

But we were always here

Fighting

For the lives of our community in the face of Aids.

For the dissolution of Section 28

The decriminalisation of homosexuality

And women's rights to live free

From violence, and with bodily autonomy

We fought

For the right to live and love with dignity

We fought for equality

And today

We were celebrated

And we were goddesses

And we were going down in fucking herstory

This bunch of lesbians

Singing mash-ups of Lady Gaga and Wagner

Lady Gagner, yaaaas

And we were on top of the fucking world.

And as we stood there in that moment

Just us

Just our little choir

The power of it all

Surged through us like electricity

They start singing – a mash-up of Lady Gaga and Wagner of course! Something that is rousing and fun and beautiful and romantic but has an undercurrent of danger…

And we don't know when exactly it happened

But it was hot

And maybe someone shouldn't have worn a fleece

Or plaid

Or leather

But someone was hot

We were all hot

After all, it was June

And at some point

In between tunes

Someone removed an outer garment

Revealing a T-shirt underneath

That bore an unfortunate semblance

With the T-shirts worn by the transphobic lesbian protesters

Who had kicked up a fuss earlier that very same day

We don't know

And cannot say

If the T-shirt wearer

Who was one of us

Was also one of them.

A T-shirt which said:

'Lesbian: A woman who loves women.'

She said:

'It was innocent'

'She meant no harm'

But harm was done

And photographs were taken

And social media acted with the swiftness of

Lesbians falling in love

That by the time the song

Drew to an end

We were being waved off stage

By the organiser

Cutting short our set.

Scene Two

July. Only CONNIE *and* LORI *have shown up for choir. They sit in chairs, amidst the mugs which are still out to catch the drips.*

LORI. Think we should give up?

CONNIE. I like to have faith.

LORI. We can't have a choir with just us.

CONNIE. I say keep on trucking, same way we always have. (*A beat.*) Let's give it ten minutes. And if no one else arrives…

LORI. I'll buy you a tonic.

They wait another moment. They hear someone approach, but the footsteps soon fade.

Why don't you drink, Connie?

CONNIE. Because I would use it to hide. And we shouldn't have to hide, should we?

LORI. No.

CONNIE. Where's your missus this evening?

LORI. I don't know.

CONNIE. Everything alright?

LORI. I told her I didn't want to move for her new job. So she's annoyed. At me. At the choir. Everything.

CONNIE. I see.

Beat.

LORI. Have you heard anything from the Pride organisers?

CONNIE. Yes. They've banned us from performing again.

LORI. Banned us?!

CONNIE. They need to be seen to take this seriously. I tried to tell them we've always welcomed trans members but they didn't want to hear it.

LORI. That's so unfair, can't we appeal?

The door opens and ANA *walks in.*

You came?

ANA. I'm here as an ally for Brig.

LORI. She isn't here.

ANA. Along with everyone else I see.

CONNIE. Nothing in the what's up group?

ANA. WhatsApp, Connie, WhatsApp.

LORI. Just Fi. She said she's running late.

ANA *is scrolling through her phone.*

ANA. This is a nightmare. This shit online is endless. And now it looks like I'm associated with it!

LORI. Oh who cares about / online /

ANA. / I care! / I have a professional reputation –

FI *comes in but has no one to help her up the steps.*

FI. / Hello? /

She waits but they don't hear her.

ANA. I've already had a terse email from the university asking me to clarify my position!

FI (*louder*). Still no ramp then!?

CONNIE. Sorry, Fi, coming.

CONNIE *rushes to help her.*

FI. Well, news of the day – there's a big thread about us on Mumsnet.

CONNIE. On Mumsnet?

ANA. Oh no.

LORI. What does it say?

FI. They're all expressing solidarity with us.

ANA. Gets worse by the minute.

FI. I do think it's all a bit unfair.

CONNIE. Have you heard from Brig, Fi?

FI. We went on one date, we're not married!

CONNIE. Sorry, I just thought –

LORI. Where's Ellie?

FI *is cut short as* BRIG *clatters in, perhaps she drops something, or slams the door. She looks dishevelled and upset – unlike her usual jolly self.*

BRIG. Sorry. (*A beat.*) Hi.

CONNIE. Glad to see you, Brig, come join us, come join us please!

FI. Yes do! And look, I even brought us a pick-me-up. (*She pulls out a bottle of vodka.*) Thought we could all use it after the car crash that was Pride.

BRIG *doesn't respond.* FI *picks a mug off the ground, tips the water out of it and fills it with vodka.*

ANA. You okay, Brig?

BRIG. Yes, fine.

CONNIE. Okay. Lovely. Well, we've got the numbers now, so let's push on with a practice, shall we? Nothing like a sing song to cheer us up.

LORI. Shouldn't we wait for Ellie and Dina?

ANA. No!

CONNIE. Has anyone heard from them?

They all shake their head.

Well, if you all get out your music, we can make a start and do what we do best, hey?

FI *passes the bottle around, though only* BRIG *and* LORI *accept a drink.*

LORI. There are just four of us, Connie –

CONNIE. We've made do with even fewer members in the past. Quick warm-up, shall we, and then we can launch into one of our favourites.

They grumblingly oblige.

LAAAAAAAA

CHORUS. LAAAAA

CONNIE. LAA LAA LAA LAA LAA

CHORUS. LAA LAA LAA LAA LAA

CONNIE. SHAA SHAA SHAA SHAA SHAAA

CHORUS. SHAA SHAA SHAA SHAA SHAAA

CONNIE. FA FA FA FA FA FA FA

CHORUS. FA FA FA FA FA FA

BRIG. FUCK FUCK FUCK FUCK FUCK.

CONNIE. Sorry?

BRIG. Sorry.

CONNIE. Are you okay?

BRIG. Yes, yes. I'm fine. Let's just get back to singing.

CONNIE. Okay – are you sure?

BRIG. Absolutely

She takes another swig.

CONNIE. Alright then, shall we start with the Dusty?

They nod and get out their sheets.

Three, four –

They begin to sing a doleful version of 'You Don't Own Me' by Dusty Springfield. They get some way into the song, but BRIG can't handle it and breaks out of the choir formation, so that the choir comes to a halt.

BRIG. I'm sorry, I'm sorry. I just don't seem able to sing today.

FI. Yeah. This sucks. We suck.

She tops up her mug.

CONNIE. Come on, that's not the spirit

FI. Oh it is very much a spirit.

LORI. What's the point. You should tell them about Pride, Connie.

FI. What about Pride?

LORI. We've been banned.

FI. What?

CONNIE. Yes.

LORI. For life.

FI. I've never heard something so stupid! Bet this wouldn't have happened if we were a gay choir.

She starts to laugh and now begins to drink heavily, straight from the bottle.

LORI. Couldn't she write a statement or something? Or an apology?

ANA. We should throw her out. Tell the Pride organisers she can't sing any more.

CONNIE. We're not throwing anyone out. As long as she wants to be one of us, she's one of us.

ANA. So much for zero tolerance.

LORI. She said it was an accident. It's an easy mistake. We both saw her T-shirt and didn't notice.

ANA. I didn't see it!

LORI. Yes you did, she showed us!

ANA. I wasn't looking. You were the one who said she looked great in it! Maybe if you weren't so busy flirting!

LORI. I wasn't flirting. I just thought it was a normal Pride T-shirt.

ANA (*disbelievingly*). Lesbian: a woman who loves a woman?

FI. I still don't get what's wrong with that.

ANA. It's the subtext –those idiotic protesters were trying to imply that trans women aren't women. Where did she even get it?

LORI. She said they were selling them that morning near the station.

ANA. And she had no idea who they were? What they stood for?

LORI. I really don't think so.

ANA. This is typical of this choir. The gendered language, the constant mockery of bisexuals.

CONNIE. I guess we're forgoing practice today, then.

LORI. She didn't mean any harm and you know it.

ANA. Well, harm's been done. Isn't that right, Brig?

    BRIG *is noticeably silent – she's not sure she has the energy for this.*

LORI. Look if she was here, I'm sure she'd –

ANA. Where is she then?

LORI. I haven't seen her since Ellie took her home after Pride. Neither of them are replying to my messages.

ANA. She's just another TERF.

LORI. Dina? A trans exclusionary radical feminist? Ha! Not sure about radical feminist.

ANA. And that's alright is it? Stop defending her!

CONNIE. Let's not turn on each other.

ANA. She couldn't even get her head round pronouns, could she?

FI. I don't understand the pronoun stuff either to be honest.

BRIG (*shocked, dismayed*). What?

FI. It's not that easy sometimes. When you grow up being taught one thing, then having to learn another.

ANA. There's always room to learn.

FI. I can't keep up. We're constantly lumped with new terminology and theory and identities. It's like before we even get a chance to be part of the mainstream, we're divided and subdivided, marginalised all over again.

BRIG. Wow.

ANA. The goal was never to be part of the mainstream. We should be disrupting it. It's the mainstream that oppressed us to begin with.

LORI. Wait, aren't you the one desperate to move to the countryside and have two point five babies?!

ANA. At least I'm not still in the closet.

CONNIE. I think this is the perfect time for a tea. Would anyone like one?

FI. Shut up, Connie! I don't want a tea! The fact is, there is nothing out there for us lesbians, nothing. There's a rainbow flag hanging in every high-street window, and no lesbian bar. Nowhere we can meet, or flirt, or just chat. Just H&M and Pret and Primark and –

ANA. Whose fault is that? Whose fault is it that banks and sandwiches have more pride than we do? Let's be real – did any of you even go to the lesbian bar?

FI. It was in a basement. And in case you haven't noticed, it's not that easy for me to get around actually.

FI *finishes what remains in the bottle of vodka.*

LORI. To be fair, it was kind of shit, I can totally see why no one went.

FI (*it's clear she's a bit drunk*). Well, that's the problem with lesbians.

ANA. Oh here we go.

FI. The problem with lesbians.

CONNIE. Don't, it's Pride month –

FI. The problem with lesbians.

BRIG (*bitterly*). Just let her finish.

FI. The problem with lesbians is that we have no loyalty, is that we are too into monogamy, is that we don't make enough money, the pink pound is for the gays, sex is for the gays

CONNIE. Speak for yourself.

FI. Fun is for the gays, fashion is for the gays –

LORI. I think I look alright.

FI. Socialising is for the gays. Community is for the gays. Cruising is for the gays. Hampstead Heath is for the gays.

CONNIE. What about the ladies' pond?

FI. History is for the gays, violence is for the gays, Aids is for the gays –

ANA. Are we seriously going to let her –

FI. Sympathy is for the gays, drugs are for the gays, plays are for the gays.

CONNIE. Did you see *Angels in America*?

LORI. Yeah, Ana's mum took us.

FI. Pride is for the gays. Stories are for the gays! Bars are for the gays! Music is for the gays. Reality TV is for the gays. Meanwhile lesbians are practically invisible!

ANA. Gay men are *men*, male privilege obviously!

FI. But what's out there for the lesbians?

LORI. Ikea is for the lesbians?

FI. Cruel jokes about U-hauls are for the lesbians?

LORI. Nail files are for the lesbians

ANA. I'm so not okay with this

FI. That's because you're not a real lesbian, darling, you're a bisexual.

   ANA *is hurt while* LORI *laughs.* LORI *is starting to enjoy this – and they're all a bit too drunk…*

LORI. Doc Martens are for the lesbians!

FI. Erasure through titillating porn for heterosexual men is for the lesbians

LORI. Oh electric toothbrushes –

ANA. What?!

FI. Yes, electric toothbrushes!

ANA. This is getting –

FI. Think about it, love – they vibrate?

ANA. Straight women have clitorises too. And not all women have clitorises anyway!

FI. Oh don't be a kill joy.

CONNIE (*nervously*). I've always wondered about the plural –
is it clitorises, or clitori? Perhaps cliteroseeees…

ANA. Connie?!

CONNIE. Sorry, yes – I think we can all agree that trans women
are women, and as a choir we welcome trans members and
those who identify as non-binary –

FI. I am not a terf! I do believe that trans women are women,
but I'm uncomfortable with the entire deconstruction of
gender, because what does that make me? If my identity
is built on me being a woman and loving women then the
erasure of women erases me, so I still can't see what's wrong
with that T-shirt!

CONNIE. Look, I really think this is getting out of –

FI. My body is real! Do you know how vulnerable you are when
you're a woman and you can't run away?! Don't you dare try
to tell me that my body is post-fucking-structural or whatever
it is you say! It feels really fucking real to live in, let me tell
you that!

BRIG. Trust me, I know bodies are real.

ANA. It's not about erasing women, it's about broadening our
definitions of it, Fi, can't you see that?

FI. And what if I don't want to?

ANA. Then we live in a world where we're chasing women who
don't look like a certain type of woman out of toilets, out of
shelters, out of women's health clinics, out of jobs! You think
that's okay?

FI *says nothing*.

BRIG. I have one – transphobia is for the lesbians!

FI. Oh please. You see the gays? What they do? Drag queens
are fine, making fun of femininity is fine, big stuffed tits
and arses and grotesque lipstick is all a bit of a laugh, but
throw a trans person in their midst, they run a mile. And
no one cares or does anything about them! It's the lesbians

who get shafted. There's no fuss over men's toilets, it's only women's toilets that get the shit. And don't get me started on how no one has ever bothered to fight for more disabled toilets. Does anyone care? No. I've been part of this choir how many years, and is there a ramp? NO! Why is it always women who have to share their spaces anyway? And men carry on, on one big jolly not giving a fuck who they include and exclude, while it's us who sit here wringing our hands over inclusivity and identity, bending over backwards to accommodate everyone. So what's left for us? What about us boring old-fashioned fleece-wearing lesbians who are paid up members of the National Trust, and just want a quiet life, tending to our allotments and maybe raising a child or two, or singing in a fucking lesbian choir – what is there for us? Why do we always have to have purple hair and polyamorous relationships to be part of a community? Where can we experience pride and romance and celebrate our sexuality? The rainbow umbrella doesn't cover me. I just want a space, for us, for me. But I'm INVISIBLE! (*Beat*) This choir was all I had.

A silence. BRIG*'s face is streaming with tears.*

BRIG (*initially with Herculean levels of restraint*). What good is a choir when we don't look out for each other? Inclusive. But there'll always be a hierarchy, won't there? I have stood here listening to you debate and complain about what? My humanity!? Am I invisible to you? Can you see me standing here? Aren't I a part of this choir too? This community? I thought I was! Do you know the week I've had? Do you even care? (*Losing it.*) Do any of you?!

ANA. I do!

BRIG. Jumping on a solidarity bandwagon isn't the same as putting time and love and effort into building a community. I came here ready to give you all the benefit of the doubt. It's just a stupid T-shirt, and yes, maybe a mistake. God knows how it wasn't obvious to you, Lori, what that T shirt stood for, it was bloody obvious to me! But this, Fi!? This?! How could you?

FI. Brig, I wasn't talking about you –

BRIG. Yes you were! You think someone like me calling for
  my rights, calling to be accepted, somehow takes something
  from you? Well, what does it take? What? Your safety? When
  has a trans woman ever harmed you? Your womanhood?
  How does my being a woman make you less of a woman?
  How? There's enough room for all of us. Why is it so hard to
  treat someone with dignity? And to think, I was ready to love
  someone who doesn't even want to share a bathroom with
  me.

  BRIG *leaves. A deafening silence.* FI *looks around,*
  embarrassed, knowing she's crossed a line.

FI. You're all on her side, aren't you?

CONNIE (*finally losing her shit*). THERE ARE NO SIDES.
  There should be no sides to a lesbian choir that is inclusive of
  all who want to be a part of it. That is all. There are no sides.
  There should just be harmony. Fat chance of that. It's over.
  I'm done. Practice is over. We're paid up on this space till the
  end of the month, so you're welcome to use it. But I won't be
  here. I quit. AU. REVOIR.

  She storms out.

FI. Oh god, what have I done. Brig – wait!

  FI *panics and rushes out after* BRIG *but she isn't as fast as*
  she'd like to be manoeuvring her chair.

  Will you help me please!?

  LORI *and* ANA *rush to help her down the steps and* FI *races*
  off. ANA *and* LORI *look at each other shocked.*

Scene Three

It's a week later. LORI *is waiting outside the choir space on her own, her gym bag beside her. She checks her watch, realising it's futile.* ANA *appears.*

ANA. Good workout?

LORI. What?

ANA. Said you were going to the gym? Packed a bag, asked me if I knew where your water bottle was. Did you have a good workout?

LORI. I changed my mind.

ANA. Really? Sounds like you made up some lie so you could come and sit here.

LORI. Did you follow me?

ANA. No.

LORI. Then why are you here?

ANA. I had a hunch.

LORI. How?

ANA. Because after all that, you left this at home.

She pulls a sports water bottle out of her bag and squirts it at LORI.

LORI. I knew you'd be annoyed if I said where I was going.

ANA. I'm leaving next week. This is the last weekend we have together, And you'd rather spend it sitting here, alone, than with me?

LORI. I wanted to see if anyone showed up.

ANA. You mean Dina?

LORI. I'm worried. No one's heard from her and this video is on loads of news sites.

ANA. We've been over this, she's probably just too embarrassed.

LORI. You don't know her at all.

ANA. What she did was unforgivable.

LORI. So what? Ban her from lesbian choir? And Fi too? Ban all the lesbians from lesbian choir. Rather than oh I don't know, talking to them?

ANA. If there's a Nazi at the table and ten other people sitting around talking to them, you've got a table of eleven Nazis.

LORI. Are you actually calling me a Nazi?!

A HANDYMAN *arrives singing along under his breath as his listens to music on his headphones – something like 'Total Eclipse of the Heart', or another heartbreak ballad.*

HANDYMAN (*singing*)....now and then... get a little bit lonely (*He take his headphones off and speaks to them.*) Don't mind me, just here to put in a ramp.

He pops his headphones back on and gets to work, humming along to his music as he does.

LORI. None of us are Nazis, Ana. We're just a bunch of lesbians with different struggles and views and experiences, who get together once a week to sing.

ANA. You know, I'm glad you're finally getting on board with being a lesbian –

LORI. Patronising much?

ANA. But there's more to being queer than demeaning, reductive jokes about U-hauls and toothbrushes.

LORI. Those narrow-minded lesbians might not be as clever as you, but they're my friends.

ANA. Is that why you're sitting here on your own?

The HANDYMAN *hammers in some nails.* LORI *looks at him, embarrassed.*

HANDYMAN (*singing*). Turn around, bright eyes.

LORI. Let's not fight again.

ANA. Why do you think I brought you to this choir? (*A beat.*) You never take me places and introduce me as your partner. It's always Ana. Just Ana. 'This is Ana.' I want to be your person, Lori, your partner. I want to hold your hand and kiss you in the street. I want to get invited to your nephew's christening or your sister's wedding. And one day I want to invite your family to our wedding. And I want children with you. And I want to sit with your mum as she unpacks boxes of your tiny baby clothes and tells me how adorable our baby is going to look in them. I want a life with you, Lori, but this limbo is killing me.

LORI. Don't you think I want all that too?

ANA. Do you really?

LORI. Yeah, it's just not that easy for me.

ANA. How do you know if you won't even try?

The HANDYMAN *hammers another nail in.*

LORI. Can we talk about this later?

ANA. No! I'm tired of pussyfooting round each other not talking about stuff –

LORI. Don't you get it? I am a butch black lesbian, Ana. I am constantly having to work out which parts of myself it's safe to show and which parts I have to hide. I'm too much of a girl for my colleagues, I'm too much of a boy at church, I'm too black for my customers. With my family I have to hide you, with you I have to hide my family. This choir was the first place I could even start to feel whole.

ANA. Your mother isn't stupid! How can you have a flatmate in a one-bedroom flat!? She knows about us! You don't have to hide!

LORI. You're not listening to me!

ANA. You don't want your family to meet me because you're cowering in a closet, ashamed of who you are.

LORI. Dragging someone out of the closet while not understanding the complexities of their culture is racist.

ANA. Don't lecture me about racism.

LORI. Oh no sorry, that's literally your job, isn't it?

HANDYMAN (*singing*)....now I'm only fallin' apart – na na na na na, total eclipse of the heart.

ANA. Why are you with me? If I'm such a racist, patronising partner, why are you even with me? Why are you stringing me along? And now you what? Want a long-distance relationship? Do you even want to be in a relationship with me?

LORI. You're the one who wants to move!

ANA. You can tell me not to go! Tell me not to go, Lori. Tell me to stay. Tell me that you can't bear to be without me. Tell me you love me and you don't know how you'll do it, and you don't want me to leave. Beg me to stay, Lori, beg me to stay for you, and I will. (*Beat.*) Lori?

LORI. I can't.

ANA. What?

LORI. I can't be in this relationship any more.

ANA. Lori.

LORI. I think you'll be happier without me.

ANA. Are you breaking up with me?

LORI. I think so, yeah. Go to Exeter. I'm sure you'll love it.

ANA. Lori!

LORI. You can stay in the flat till you move. I'll crash at my mum's.

LORI *leaves, past the* HANDYMAN *who watches her go. Maybe he pulls out his earphones and watches the end of this drama with interest.* ANA *calls after her.*

ANA. Oh right, what will you tell her? That you broke up with your flatmate?!

ANA starts to cry, but is acutely aware of the HANDYMAN *watching her. He slowly begins to approach her, and she turns pointedly away, she doesn't want to have to speak to him. He continues his cautious approach, until he reaches her, she still ignoring him entirely.*

Just leave me alone! – Oh.

He hands her a handkerchief. She looks at it hesitantly.

HANDYMAN. It's clean.

She takes it and blows her nose.

Boy trouble? Not all of us are wankers, I promise. Cheer up. Sure the right one's out there for you somewhere.

ANA (*swallowing her irritation, handing back the handkerchief*). Thank you.

HANDYMAN. You can keep that.

She leaves and he goes back to his music and continues to install the ramp.

Scene Four

At the choir venue. FI *comes into the hall – the ramp has finally been installed.*

FI. Now there's a ramp.

She waits. No one shows up. She makes a phone call –

(*Hopefully.*) Brig? (*Realising it's voicemail.*) Fucking voicemail. Fucking… argh.

She hangs up. She sings/plays a bit of a song.

ACT FOUR

Scene One

LORI *arrives at* DINA*'s house. She fiddles with her phone and then puts her phone in her pocket before ringing the bell.* DINA*'s husband opens the door.*

LORI. Oh hi.

HUSBAND. Cable guy, right? Or I should say cable girl.

LORI. Yeah.

HUSBAND. I didn't ask for you.

LORI. Um, so it's just a routine follow-up visit our company does to make sure everything is to your satisfaction and working as it should.

The HUSBAND *looks suspicious but accepts this.*

HUSBAND. Come in.

LORI *enters, the door shuts.*

LORI. We usually get a pre-arranged time in, but the number on the file, I think your wife's, we tried the number several times, but it seems to have been disconnected, our records show.

HUSBAND. Uh-huh.

LORI. And my manager said I should just drop by on my way home after a shift to check everything was in order anyway.

HUSBAND. It's through there.

LORI *goes to fiddle with the connection, and ostensibly check it, but really looking for signs of* DINA.

LORI. Your wife not home, then?

HUSBAND. No.

LORI. Ah. Does she have a new number or something?

HUSBAND. Yes.

> LORI *carries on working, and thinking how to find out if* DINA*'s alright.*

> You know, while you're here can you look at the connection in the bathroom? I can't seem to get all the channels I have in here on there.

LORI. Sure, let me take a look.

HUSBAND. Through here.

> LORI *exits off into a bathroom.* HUSBAND *stays outside, on stage.*

> It's my favourite place to watch TV from. The bath.

LORI (*popping her head back in*). Oh yeah, like a fish, haha.

HUSBAND. Like a shark.

LORI (*disappearing off again*). So, where's she gone? Your wife.

HUSBAND. Oh. holiday.

LORI (*from off*). Somewhere nice?

HUSBAND. No one goes somewhere not nice on holiday.

LORI (*from off*). Ha, yeah course. And the kids?

HUSBAND (*starting to get suspicious*). With her.

> LORI *re-enters.*

LORI. Cool, that's cool. Sorry I chat too much, people are always telling me I chat too much.

HUSBAND. So what do you think is best? For this connection?

LORI. Yeah, so you want your satellite channels on this, right?

HUSBAND. Yeah?

LORI. Right so I'm going to have to take a look upstairs if that's okay, see if there's a good access point for a satellite cable.

HUSBAND. You want to go upstairs?

LORI. Yeah. That okay?

HUSBAND. Sure.

LORI. Do you want to show me up?

HUSBAND. That's fine – I'm sure you'll find your way. (*Beat.*) I have nothing to hide.

LORI. You'd be surprised. One time, this old white lady was growing weed all over her basement. She tried to give me a bag but I'm not into that stuff. See you in a sec.

LORI goes upstairs. Meanwhile DINA's husband checks something on his phone, scrolls, grimaces – we vaguely hear the sound of the Ministry of Lesbian Affairs performing at Pride. He looks upstairs to where LORI is, realising who she is. LORI comes back down.

Okay so I'm going to have to come back another time for that job, maybe you can let me know a good time? Maybe when your wife is back?

HUSBAND. Uh-huh.

LORI. When do you think that'll be?

HUSBAND. Next month.

LORI. That's nice. You must miss her. You couldn't go with her?

HUSBAND. I'm the breadwinner. She's the breadmaker.

LORI. Gotcha. Well, I can just make a note in the calendar to give her a call then – is this the right number on file still?

She shows him her tablet screen.

HUSBAND. Hey – you like music?

LORI. What?

HUSBAND. Music. Singing. That sort of thing.

LORI. Umm...

He plays King Princess's 'Pussy is God' that the choir sang at Pride. LORI *knows the game is up.*

HUSBAND. You like this song?

LORI. Um, I don't think I know it.

HUSBAND. You don't know this song?

LORI. Don't think so.

HUSBAND. Are you sure?

LORI. Positive.

HUSBAND. Really? This song? Listen closer.

LORI. Nope! Right, well, thanks for that. I will get back –

HUSBAND. Shut up, you dyke –

He pushes her up against a wall roughly, pinning her hard as she struggles against his strength.

What are you doing here?

LORI. Where is she?

HUSBAND. I don't think you're in a position to be asking any questions, do you?

LORI. Let me go or I'll yell.

HUSBAND. Make a sound and I'll break your neck. Maybe you're a burglar breaking in. You look like a boy, don't you? Maybe I should call the police.

LORI. What have you done with her?

HUSBAND. You know, if you just wore a bit of make-up you might even be passable as a girl.

She kicks his shin and he howls in pain. She tries to escape but stumbles over him and falls to the floor, hitting her forehead. He pins her down again.

You shouldn't have done that. You really shouldn't have done that.

LORI's *phone beeps – the five-minute warning.*

Who's that? Your girlfriend or something?

LORI (*scoffs confidently, knowing she's got an out*). Fuck you.

He realises that she's probably told someone where she's going and he can't get away with hurting her. Defeated, reining in his rage, he lets her go. Besides, he has one more trump card – DINA. LORI scrambles to her feet, and touches her bleeding forehead.

HUSBAND. Get the fuck out of here. And don't bother coming to look for her again. You won't find her.

He smiles coldly. LORI leaves.

Scene Two

ANA *teaches a class at her new university.*

ANA. When we read bell hooks' *Teaching Community: A Pedagogy of Hope*, we are presented with a counterpoint to the fractured, unreliable and often hopeless subjectivity of post-modernist post-structuralism. 'Dominator culture has tried to keep us all afraid,' she writes. 'To make us choose safety instead of risk, sameness instead of diversity. Moving through that fear, finding out what connects us, revelling in our differences; this is the process that brings us closer, that gives us a world of shared values… (*Her voice cracks but she perseveres.*) …of meaningful community.' (*She is about to cry.*) I'm sorry, I just need – a moment. Excuse me.

She leaves her class to compose herself.

Scene Three

BRIG *is at home, singing along to something like 'Positions'
by Ariana Grande, cooking and getting into the song. Over the
music we hear a buzzer. She realises it's someone at her door.
She goes to see –* LORI *busts in, still bleeding, straight from*
DINA*'s house.*

LORI. Sorry, sorry, I didn't know where to – what to – he's
done something to her. He's sent her somewhere or hurt her, I
don't know what but I –

BRIG. 'Hi Brig, how are you? Haven't heard from you in a long
time, are you okay?'

LORI. Sorry, sorry. I'm sorry. (*Beat.*) Didn't you get my
messages?

BRIG. I did. Did you notice I hadn't replied?

A beat.

What are you doing here?

LORI. I was just at Dina's and – and – I remembered you lived
here.

BRIG. And you thought what? That we'd sit down to dinner?
Watch a film?

LORI. Sorry, I didn't know where else to go, or what to do. It's
– it's Dina.

BRIG. Dina! I thought you'd come to apologise.

LORI. I am sorry, I am. I really am. I don't know what else to
say.

BRIG. Sometimes apologies aren't enough, I suppose.

LORI. I went over to Dina's place, because no one's heard from
her. So I went over and only her husband was there –

BRIG. That was incredibly stupid.

LORI. No trace of her anywhere, no toothbrush, no clothes, no kids. I think, I can't be sure, but I think he's sent her and the kids back to Qatar. You're a lawyer, aren't you? Could you help? Could you help get her back? Maybe like an asylum thing or – or –

BRIG. I'm not an immigration lawyer.

LORI. But maybe you know someone who could help?

BRIG. Look, I just want a bit of space from that choir.

LORI. She could be in danger.

BRIG (*sighs*). I'll ask around, but if we have no way of getting in touch with her, and she hasn't attempted to contact anyone, then I'm not sure there's much we can do – (*Notices* LORI*'s bleeding forehead.*) Are you bleeding?

LORI. Oh –

BRIG. What happened?

LORI. He just roughed me up a bit to scare me. I'm okay.

BRIG *looks at it closely.*

BRIG. It's quite a gash. Here, sit down.

LORI *sits.* BRIG *goes to fetch a first-aid kit. She returns, and sits down beside* LORI.

Let me see.

She dabs the cut with some TCP and cotton wool. LORI *hisses with pain.*

LORI. Stings a bit.

BRIG. You're okay. Don't think it'll need a stitch.

LORI. You some kind of expert?

BRIG. You're not the only queer in this joint to get beaten up, you know. Okay otherwise? No other cuts or bumps?

LORI. Yeah. Just shook up, I guess.

BRIG. Is there someone you want me to call? Ana?

LORI. We... broke up.

BRIG. And your family? Your mum?

LORI. No, I don't want her to see me like this. Put her through enough already.

BRIG. What do you mean?

LORI *shrugs, tries not to cry.*

What, by being gay? Sweetheart. This isn't your fault. You hear me? We don't choose these things.

LORI. Wish I'd never gone to that stupid choir. Feel like it's ruined all of our lives.

BRIG. That's a bit dramatic.

LORI. It's true. Dina would still be okay, Ana and I would still be together, you wouldn't have had to put up with all that shit. It ruined everything.

BRIG. I think things will feel differently in a little while.

LORI. Seriously. It's no wonder lesbians shack up and disappear. It's just easier to keep yourself to yourself, grow vegetables, rescue cats, do DIY around the house. And not face the world.

BRIG. I can see how you feel that today.

LORI. Well, don't you? Don't you just want to hide away?

BRIG. Sometimes.

LORI. How do you do it, then? How are you so positive?

BRIG. I don't always feel positive. That's when you need to fight the hardest.

LORI. What's the point, we'll never win.

BRIG. The point? The point, Lori, is if we don't fight for ourselves, for each other, who will? Whether you like it or not we are all in this ring together, and we are fighting for our lives.

A beat as LORI *absorbs this.*

LORI. I'm sorry I didn't fight for you.

   BRIG *sighs, she knows* LORI *needs a friend.*

BRIG. Do you want to sleep here tonight?

   LORI *nods.*

   I'll go get you some bedding.

   BRIG *gets up to fetch the bedding.*

LORI. Brig?

BRIG. Mm?

LORI. Love you.

BRIG. You are such a lesbian.

   Blackout.

Scene Four

Back in the hall which has evidently flooded at some point.
CONNIE *comes in, flips the lights. They flicker on for a
moment, short circuit and go out. She tries the switch a few
times, but nothing.*

CONNIE. Oh bugger. Ridiculous. Absolutely ridiculous.

   *She pops her purse down and heads to the kitchen and rifles
   around for some candles. She fishes some out of the cupboard
   and starts to light them.* FI *comes in but* CONNIE *doesn't
   notice.*

FI. Looks like shit in here.

CONNIE (*startled*). Fi! Sorry, you startled me. You came.

FI. Long time no see, hey? What's with the candles?

CONNIE. Power's out. There was a flood.

FI. How biblical. Isn't there someone you can call?

CONNIE. Strictly speaking, we're not allowed to be in here. The building's been closed down.

FI. How did you get in?

CONNIE. Silver lining of terrible management is that no one ever asked for the keys back. Would you believe the ramp's in!

FI. It's been here a while.

CONNIE. Thank you for coming.

FI. It'll be nice to see everyone again. If they turn up.

CONNIE. Lori promised she'd bring her van.

FI. I didn't know the piano was yours.

CONNIE. I donated it back when I started the choir. But now (*Crossly.*) I'm un-donating it.

CONNIE *looks around – there are some sodden boxes of music books*

I suppose I can take these too.

FI. Smells of old towels in here.

CONNIE (*about the books as she leafs through one*). Ruined, these are ruined.

FI. It's bloody freezing in here, isn't it? Guess no power means no tea.

CONNIE. 'Fraid not.

FI. What's happening to this place? Will they fix it up?

CONNIE. Imagine they'll sell it. Turn it into flats.

LORI *enters.*

LORI. Hey!

CONNIE. Oh good, I was beginning to worry.

LORI. Parked up outside but it only gives you twenty minutes so we've got to be quick.

FI (*shyly*). Hi Lori.

LORI. Hey, Fi. You alright?

ELLIE *enters*.

ELLIE. You call for some muscle?

FI. Ellie!

ELLIE *hugs* FI.

ELLIE. Hey, my lezzers, you miss me?

FI. Yes!

ELLIE. Wow candlelight, very romantic!

FI. Where've you been, then?

LORI. Yeah, you were totally MIA. Silent meditation retreat or something?

ELLIE. Just needed to take some time out, focus on me, Ellie's needs and all. Went to some SLA meetings.

FI. Sla?

ELLIE. Sex and love addiction. What can I say, it's a problem. But I've been abstinent sixty-four days and counting.

LORI. And Dina? Heard anything?

ELLIE. No. She totally ghosted me a week after Pride. But hey, at least her dropping me was my one-way ticket to rock bottom.

LORI. I spoke to Brig by the way. She said she still needs some space but was going to think about it.

Everyone sighs a little sadly.

Shall we take a look at this piano, then?

LORI *attempts to push it – the castors have broken and it won't budge.*

Yep. The wheels have come off. Maybe if a few of us push?

ELLIE. Lemme help.

They both try to push it, with no luck. CONNIE *gets in too, nothing. They give it all they've got when* ANA *walks in.*

ANA. Hey

LORI *falls over from the shock and effort.*

Are you okay?

LORI. What are you doing here?

ANA. Connie said she needed help.

CONNIE. I messaged the whole WhatsApp group.

LORI. But you live five hours away.

ELLIE. Well, it's not budging so it's probably a wasted trip.

ANA. Actually, Lori, when I moved I realised I took your dolly.

LORI. You've got my dolly?!

ANA. Sorry – it's in the car – I'll go get it.

She leaves.

ELLIE. You have a dolly?

LORI. You don't?

FI. You are so gay.

ANA *comes back in with a dolly.*

LORI. I can't believe you stole my dolly.

ANA. Least it's coming in useful now!

LORI. I was looking for it everywhere.

ELLIE. I should get a dolly.

CONNIE. Now how shall we do this?

FI. If you each get a corner, I think there are handles on the back, and then from the front you can hold it just under the keyboard, see?

They listen as FI *takes charge.*

Alright – on three, lift and move to the left

ELLIE. Whose left?

FI. My left! And then gently place it down onto the dolly. Got it? One, two –

LORI. Wait so is it on three? Or after three?

ELLIE. I think it's after three –

ANA. It's not like singing, it's not like come in after three –

ELLIE. Well, excuse me –

They all chatter at once – their various interpretations of this, until FI *cuts through the chatter.*

FI. QUIET! You lift ON three. Got it? ON three.

CONNIE. Okay.

FI. One two THREE!

They all heave the piano up and attempt to move it onto the dolly.

ELLIE. Hey, now most of us are here, I wanted to make some amends. Fi, Ana – I'm sorry I hooked up with both of you.

LORI. What?

FI. Ellie!

ELLIE. And, Lori – sorry I got with your bird –

ANA. Oh my god.

LORI. Oh my god.

ELLIE. I mean you'd broken up by then but still, I went over to help her move, and one thing led to another –

ANA. It wasn't like that, we just hugged!

CONNIE. Could we please focus on the task at hand!

ANA. The dolly just won't stay still.

They put the piano down again, defeated.

ELLIE. But, yeah I want you to know, I was acting out of my own loneliness and shame and lack of self-esteem, so I'm sorry.

FI, LORI *and* ANA *mutter – 'it's okay', and 'thanks'.*

CONNIE. This isn't working.

LORI. We need another person to hold the dolly.

FI. I could try?

They haven't noticed but BRIG *has walked in.*

BRIG. I'll do it.

They all look up, in shock, then all speak at once –

LORI. Brig!

CONNIE. Oh you came!

ANA. Are you alright?

ELLIE. You never replied to my amend!

FI. Brig –

The choir hear FI *and quieten down.*

I've been trying to call you. I wanted to see you. Those things I said – I didn't mean to hurt you, I really didn't. I – I miss you.

BRIG (*ignores her*). I actually came because I have some news that I thought everyone might want to hear. (*Beat.*) About Dina.

ELLIE. Dina?

LORI. Oh my god, you've heard from her?

CONNIE. Is she alright?

ELLIE. What? Is she okay?

BRIG. If you'll let me [finish] – I've been in touch with a cousin of hers in Berlin. She doesn't have access to a phone or the internet, but as far as he could tell from the chat with extended family, it seems she's in Qatar and okay for now.

ELLIE. What the fuck? I had no idea!

LORI. Okay for now? What does that mean?

BRIG. I don't know what that means exactly. But the cousin thinks he might be able to get her out. And a friend of mine, who's an immigration lawyer, is trying to sort things this end. But it's a long road and there are no guarantees.

ELLIE. Shit.

ANA. If there's anything we can do?

BRIG. I'll let you know if there is.

LORI. Hope she's okay.

ELLIE. Yeah.

BRIG. Me too.

This settles with the choir.

BRIG. Come on then, let's get this piano moved.

FI. Brig, please. I'm so sorry, I was drunk, and hurting and – and… I don't know what else to say. Do you think we could ever be friends again?

BRIG. No.

A painful pause.

Not yet.

ANA. I have a thought. How about a song?

CONNIE. That's a nice idea!

BRIG. I'd rather just get this done and head off if that's alright.

ANA. Sure, yes of course.

ELLIE. Yeah I gotta call my sponsor.

LORI. And I'm gonna get a ticket if we wait any longer. Let's just get a move on.

The choir resigns to this, the glimmer of hope, shot.

ELLIE. How many dykes does it take to steal a piano, am I right?

CONNIE. We're not stealing it, it's mine!

ELLIE. No shit, really?

CONNIE. It belonged to my wife. And as there's no use for it here any more, clearly, I want it back.

BRIG. You're married, Connie?

CONNIE. I was.

ANA. I didn't know that!

LORI. Why didn't you ever say anything?

CONNIE. Some things are hard to talk about.

FI. Divorce is tough –

CONNIE. She died.

BRIG. What? When?

CONNIE. Some years ago. Emelda was the love of my life for thirty years, and my wife for two months. She died soon after it became legal to get married.

LORI. Oh my god! Connie!

CONNIE. That's when I started the choir. I thought I told you all this?

FI. No!

CONNIE. Yes, well, the choir gave me something to do. Or rather somewhere I could still feel like I was with family. We never had children, you see. And our own families – well, it was much harder in those times. All we had was each other. So if you don't mind, I would quite like this piano back.

A pause as everyone takes this in.

BRIG. Alright. One song.

CONNIE. Really?

BRIG *nods*.

Oh Brig, that means the world. Before we – just one more thing. Sometimes we make mistakes, god knows I've made many. And sometimes we let each other down terribly. But that's what families do isn't it? And you are my family. (*A pause, she fetches some soggy books.*) Now, if you'll indulge me a final old-fogey number, please turn to page fifty-two.

Can everyone make it out? I know it's a bit dark, and the books a bit damp but it should be familiar to you all?

BRIG (*too excitedly*). Oh I love this one! (*Then sobering up, remembering she's hurt.*)

LORI. Me too.

ANA. I do too.

FI. My book's too soggy.

CONNIE. I'm sure someone will share!

BRIG. Here.

People arrange themselves, distributing books and candles between them – there aren't enough to go round so they have to share.

CONNIE. Alright. Everyone happy to do a stumble through?

LORI. Has anyone got a spare candle? I can't see.

ANA. Here.

LORI. Thanks

CONNIE. Excellent. And remember – you sound best when???

CHORUS. We listen to each other...

CONNIE. Exactly. Alright. On four –

The song is 'Bridge Over Troubled Water' by Simon & Garfunkel. Perhaps CONNIE punctuates their singing with little reminders – 'Altos, this is your bit!' or 'From your diaphragms, remember!'

It's rousing and beautiful and healing.

Towards the end, lights up on DINA in a room in Qatar, alone, singing along. Or perhaps she just echoes the final refrain on her own.

They finish. A silence.

The End.

A Nick Hern Book

The Ministry of Lesbian Affairs first published in Great Britain as a paperback original in 2022 by Nick Hern Books Limited, The Glasshouse, 49a Goldhawk Road, London W12 8QP, in association with Soho Theatre and Damsel Productions

The Ministry of Lesbian Affairs copyright © 2022 Iman Qureshi

Iman Qureshi has asserted her right to be identified as the author of this work

Cover image: Ella Mahony

Designed and typeset by Nick Hern Books, London
Printed in Great Britain by Mimeo Ltd, Huntingdon, Cambridgeshire PE29 6XX

A CIP catalogue record for this book is available from the British Library

ISBN 978 1 83904 078 8

www.nickhernbooks.co.uk

facebook.com/nickhernbooks

twitter.com/nickhernbooks